The True Profession of the Gospel

AUGUSTUS TOPLADY
AND RECLAIMING OUR REFORMED
FOUNDATIONS

by Lee Gatiss

The Latimer Trust

ISBN 978-0-946307-74-6

Published by the Latimer Trust June 2010

The Latimer Trust (formerly Latimer House, Oxford) is a conservative Evangelical research organisation within the Church of England, whose main aim is to promote the history and theology of Anglicanism as understood by those in the Reformed tradition. Interested readers are welcome to consult its website for further details of its many activities.

The Latimer Trust
PO Box 26685, London N14 4XQ UK
Registered Charity: 1084337
Company Number: 4104465
Web: www.latimertrust.org
E-mail: administrator@latimertrust.org

"If Toplady is remembered at all today, it is probably as the author of a number of famous hymns. Yet in his own time he represented a strand of Anglicanism which sought to stand in continuity with both the Church of England's Reformation roots and the more precise articulation of Reformed Orthodoxy. In this study, Lee Gatiss does a fine job of recovering this aspect of Toplady for today, and thereby reminding his church that Latitudinarianism, Anglo-Catholicism, Liberalism, and theologically lightweight evangelicalism are not the only traditions which can lay claim to being Anglican."

Professor Carl Trueman, Professor of Historical Theology and Church History at Westminster Theological Seminary, Philadelphia.

"In this lively, stimulating, and sometimes provocative piece Lee Gatiss introduces us to a man whose words we still sing, but whose wider theology lies neglected. His focus is not, however, limited to Toplady. In the first half he makes a powerful case that the historic Church of England was Reformed in its theology. Many evangelicals today will rejoice to hear this, but then comes the twist in the tail as the writings of figures like Whitefield and Toplady himself are used to show just what it meant to be Reformed. We find, for instance, that they were thorough-going covenant theologians, committed to the idea of an eternal intratrinitarian covenant of redemption. By the end of the study we may be left feeling that others are wrong to question the place of Reformed theology in the historic Church of England, but we may also be left rather less sure that what passes for Reformed today is the same as it was in the past. I expect that readers will find this study at once encouraging and challenging. It is a strong example of the way in which historical writing can be both responsible and transparently useful for the church today."

Dr. Garry Williams, Director of The John Owen Centre, London.

Contents

AUGUSTUS TOPLADY A. B.

Photographic reproduction of an engraving in *Memoirs of the Rev. Mr. Toplady* published in 1794 by Walter Row. Thanks to Mike Pettit of www.toplady.org.uk and Edward Malcolm of *The Gospel Magazine*.

Acknowledgements

The material in this book began life as various talks for the Fellowship of Word and Spirit Conference, the Church Society Conference, and 'Learning for Life' at St. Helen's, Bishopsgate in 2009. I am very grateful for the opportunities this gave me to share material I had been reading and thinking about for some years, and for the wonderful times of fellowship and feedback which have helped greatly to improve it. These talks were then developed to become my ThM dissertation at Westminster Theological Seminary, Philadelphia (USA) under the supervision of Prof. Carl Trueman, seconded by Dr. Garry Williams at the John Owen Centre in London. My thanks go to them for their perceptive comments and encouragement and to John Richardson, Timothy Edwards, Andrew Atherstone, Marty Foord, and Dick Lucas who all made positive and useful remarks along the way, especially when they disagreed or spotted errors in the detail.

This book could not have been completed without the support and encouragement of family and friends who diligently prayed for me throughout its preparation. My warmest thanks go to Joshua for the enjoyable distraction of frequent light-sabre duels; to Cara for praying night after night for daddy's book; and to Lucy for not keeping us all up at night too much in your early months. And particularly to my wife Kerry for your generosity, patience, and sacrificial, covenant love throughout the long gestation and agonising birth of this project, affectionately referred to as our fourth child.

But most of all to my gracious saviour for whose glory alone it was written, for never giving up on an undeserving sinner and very slow learner.

"Nothing in my hand I bring, simply to thy cross I cling."

1. Anglican and Evangelical Midlife Crises

> *Where are the men who will be found so indolent that they will allow themselves to be so easily overborne and driven from their hereditary possessions? Let each look out for himself. For my own part, I should need to be completely overwhelmed by sound reasons before I parted with any portion of my heritage, and even then it would be with extreme reluctance!*
>
> - John Owen, *Biblical Theology* 5.12

Evangelicalism and Anglicanism are both experiencing something akin to a midlife crisis. People going through such crises are often prone to indulge, quite out of character, in strange and bizarre behaviour. They may experiment with something new and seemingly more exciting than their former way of life, abandoning the stability of former associations and beliefs while questioning "who am I?" No-one can deny that paroxysms of doubt and division, fuelled by lust (for illicit sex or simply money and power), have wracked both constituencies on a global scale. The result is confusion about the character of Evangelicalism and the identity of Anglicanism — who is 'in,' who is 'out,' what is authentic and what an intrusive novelty? This should be unsurprising given the levels of theological experimentation and cultural accommodation that have been tried.

What has been forgotten in the mêlée that has broken out between competing visions of the future are the stabilising roots from which Evangelicals and Anglicans have always drawn their vital spark. Whether through ignorance or neglect, they have drifted away from Reformed theology, from which their vivacity and vigour have flowed in the past. Only by a speedy recovery of their marriages to Reformed orthodoxy can further crises be averted and each tradition reinvigorated.

The primary subject of this study, Augustus Montague Toplady (1740-1778), once wrote, "Is there a single heresy, that ever annoyed the Christian world, which has not its present partisans among those who profess conformity to the Church of England?"[1] The same, of course,

---

[1] A. M. Toplady, *The Complete Works of Augustus Toplady* (Harrisonburg, Virginia: Sprinkle Publications, 1987), 275.

could be said of those who claim the now rather elastic title 'Evangelical.' Yet despite the rather tired and dreary mantra of inclusivism, that such pluriformity is the 'genius' of Anglicanism, "our particular charism" as one well-known liberal put it recently,[2] it is a sign of degeneration to be lamented rather than something to be celebrated or nurtured. Liberalism is parasitic and will ultimately suck the life out of any ecclesiastical witness to Christian truth so that it becomes little more than a pious, spiritualised veneer for worldliness and moralism. Yet this is not the metanarrative one is confronted with in the pages of the Church press, where 'tolerant' and seemingly humble doctrinal uncertainty is the order of the day, and challengers to the modernist impulse are portrayed as theological terrorists.

Bishop Tom Wright has written that, "Human life, then, can be seen as grounded in and constituted by the implicit or explicit stories which humans tell themselves and one another... When we examine how stories work in relation to other stories, we find that human beings tell stories because this is how we perceive, and indeed relate to, the world." He concludes by saying that, "Stories are, actually, peculiarly good at modifying or subverting other stories and their worldviews."[3] If he is right, then it is imperative that the myth (currently holding sway) of enlightened, modern, liberal triumph over the bigoted forces of restrictive conservatism is challenged by an alternative recitation of Church history. History is so often written by the victors as a way of manipulating their defeated opponents into accepting a new self-identity as the weak and deservedly marginalised losers. This is what coaxes many Evangelicals to leave behind the simple faith of their youth and to adopt more progressive, moderate, and seemingly 'generous' views. The ambitious 'appreciate their Evangelical heritage' of course, but by sidelining, watering down, or supplementing it from elsewhere they are able to join the ranks of the elite. In time they also swallow and perpetuate the subversive story which led to their own elevation. Once they have gained entry into the 'inner circle,' too often they willingly connive at the marginalisation of those with whom they were formerly associated.

The Reformed tradition within Evangelicalism and within Anglicanism has been too long marginalised by such tactics. And yet it is this tradition that holds the key to the true character, genius, and identity

---

[2] Giles Fraser, "Are you Anglican or C of E?" *Church Times* No. 7637 (London, 31 July 2009), 9.

[3] N. T. Wright, *The New Testament and the People of God* (London: SPCK, 1992), 38, 40.

of both. In a previous generation it was *de rigueur* for a man like John Stott to say of Anglicanism that, "according to its own formularies, this church is reformed and evangelical."[4] He was on safe and solid ground in affirming this, since at her Coronation, Queen Elizabeth II promised to maintain, to the utmost of her power, "the true profession of the gospel... the Protestant Reformed religion." Yet it is to be doubted whether, if this phrase is even retained for the next coronation, there will be many in the church who still maintain that form of Christian belief. More recently such confidence in the faith of our forefathers has seemingly vanished so that the Thirty-nine Articles of Religion can be spoken of by observers as a "thorn in the flesh" for the Church of England which only "extreme Protestants" have a bad habit of remembering.[5] A global attempt to make the Anglican Communion merely *Christian* again (without distinctively Evangelical and Reformed emphases such as justification by faith *alone*) is seen by many as a great spiritual advance, on a par with the eighteenth century revivals.[6]

In historical perspective this reveals just how much ground has been lost. Co-belligerence in the face of aggressive liberal intolerance is not necessarily a bad thing, though it has its dangers if not kept in proper perspective.[7] The goalposts appear to have moved substantially with seemingly little recognition of how or why. Beyond Anglicanism, it is also now perfectly respectable to accept the label Evangelical while rejecting cardinal tenets of the faith of previous generations of Evangelicals, such as the unerring nature of the Bible and the precious doctrine of penal substitutionary atonement. Alliances easily forged in time of need can become insidiously corrupting.

Paul David Tripp says that "The disorientation of midlife is the result of the collision of a *powerful personal awareness* and a *powerful*

---

[4] J. R. W. Stott, *Christ the Controversialist: The Basics of Belief* (Leicester: IVP, 1996 [1970]), 8.

[5] M. Furlong, *C of E: The State It's In* (London: Hodder and Stoughton, 2000), 57, 78.

[6] I refer of course to the Fellowship of Confessing Anglicans (FCA) which sprang from the Global Anglican Futures Conference (GAFCON) in Jerusalem in 2008. This is based on the so-called Jerusalem Declaration, which apart from containing too many nods in the direction of Anglo-Catholicism, also deliberately omitted the "alone" from its declaration about justification by faith.

[7] On the dangers of tolerating liberalism see my *Christianity and the Tolerance of Liberalism: J. Gresham Machen and the Presbyterian Controversy of 1922-1937* (London: Latimer Trust, 2008).

personal interpretation."[8] The more we realise the depth of our current crises, the more it seems as if midlife has come crashing down on Anglicanism and Evangelicalism. Reinstalling Reformed theology as the basic operating system for both Anglicanism and Evangelicalism would go a long way towards correcting the imbalances we are experiencing. There must also be a recognition that such globally connected systems are always open to attack from the theological equivalent of computer viruses, worms, or Trojan horses. Such quirks ought never to be accepted as 'normal' and left to their own nefarious devices.

The question also presents itself as to whether Reformed believers consider themselves as mainstream or extreme. Are we part of the core of what it means to be Evangelical or Anglican or merely a militant tendency seeking to subvert the true nature of the organisations we have 'infiltrated'? The Reformed may feel they are one while being widely portrayed as the other, with quite disorientating and discouraging effects. We need to recover a confidence in where we came from.

In a similar way, Tripp writes that midlife reveals the heart's ruling desires and exposes any gaps between a person's confessional theology and their functional theology. Under pressure we are compelled to recognise the gaps between what we say we believe and what we actually do. Discrepancies here can lead to anger, bitterness, loss of identity, and "a flagging of meaning and purpose."[9] Not wanting to stretch the analogy too far, the recent history of Anglicanism and Evangelicalism certainly exhibits these theological gaps and destructive symptoms. The antidote, naturally, is to bring our functional theology back into line with confessional theology, which means a wholehearted return to the source of Anglican and Evangelical clarity in Reformational teaching on the doctrines of grace. There are signs that this may be happening in many places; the New Calvinism of the 'young, restless, and Reformed,' for example, came in third in *Time* magazine's list of the most influential world-changing movements in March 2009.[10]

This book looks back to another moment in time when a resurgence of what is sometimes disparagingly called Calvinism brought

---

[8] P. D. Tripp, *Lost in the Middle: Midlife and the Grace of God* (Wapwallopen, PA: Shepherd Press, 2004), 33; emphasis original.

[9] Tripp, *Lost in the Middle*, 50-51.

[10] "10 Ideas Changing the World Right Now," *Time*, March 12, 2009. See also C. Hansen, *Young, Restless, Reformed: A Journalist's Journey with the New Calvinists* (Wheaton, IL: Crossway, 2008).

revival to the churches. There were also great divisions within the new movement itself and within existing denominations. Alongside this renewed vitality there was also a determined effort to overturn the ruling paradigm in ecclesiastical history. The Church of England was seen as a latitudinarian melting pot of various contradictory persuasions. Reformed theology had been presented as a menace to the peace of both the Church and the Evangelical movement. So Reformed Evangelical writers sought to put the record straight. My intention is to examine their background and role in the eighteenth century revivals and their handling of the clash with Arminianism. Yet I hope not merely to examine them but also in some degree to imitate them, so that my retelling of the story (like theirs) will subvert the inaccurate, corrupting, and sometimes paralysing version which currently passes for orthodoxy in many circles. If this serves to inspire or empower others to survive the midlife identity crisis and plough on in God's grace to recover our lost heritage, in this way I hope (as Toplady said) to contribute, though ever so little, to the return of the ark.

2. A Brief History of the Anglican Reformed Tradition

> *I have taken care to satisfy every unprejudiced person, that that which we now call Calvinism, is to be found in the writings of the ancient fathers of the Church, and is the very doctrine which the first reformers of our own Church professed, and maintained, and which is contained in our Articles, Homilies and liturgy, and which our Archbishops and Bishops, and the whole body of our English clergy have generally asserted and vindicated.*
>
> - John Edwards, *Veritas Redux: Evangelical Truths Restored* (1707)

2.1. *The Reformed Reformation*

Dean Inge is reputed to have said once that, "A religion without a history is a nervous disorder." However depressed those of Reformed convictions in the Church of England or in Evangelicalism today might be, their theological position is by no means novel or disordered. Indeed, the origins of both can be shown to rest on distinctively Reformed foundations. After Henry VIII's decisive break with Rome, the first century of the new Protestant establishment was a period of immense success and prosperity for Reformed theology in Britain; as Jonathan Moore has reiterated recently, "England and Scotland were the only kingdoms in the sixteenth century in which the Reformed faith was established as the national religion."[11] This is due to the fact that it was men of Reformed convictions who reformed the church and held her highest and most influential offices. As W. H. Griffith Thomas says, "the English Reformers were all what is understood as 'Calvinists'; and, indeed, until the time of Archbishop Laud no other doctrine was known in the Anglican Church."[12]

The Thirty-nine Articles, the Book of Common Prayer, and the

---

[11] J. D. Moore, *English Hypothetical Universalism: John Preston and the Softening of Reformed Theology* (Cambridge: Eerdmans, 2007), 223.

[12] W. H. Griffith Thomas, *The Principles of Theology: An Introduction to the Thirty-nine Articles* (London: Vine Books, 1930), 243.

Homilies all witness to the success of Reformed theology in England. It was not, as some have tried to make it seem, as if the Calvinist puritans were a theologically extreme bunch, out of touch with a more moderate establishment. No, the doctrines of grace *were* the established religion. There was a widespread Reformed consensus and, says Moore, "a firm conviction that salvation is by predestinating grace and not the grace of sacramentalism, and that therefore the Church of Rome is to be abhorred, and every resurgence of its ceremonialism to be fiercely resisted."[13] It was for holding to the *Reformed* (non-Lutheran, non-Zwinglian, Protestant) doctrine of the sacraments that men like Nicholas Ridley and Thomas Cranmer were martyred, this Reformed sacramentology being one of the "twin pivots of the Doctrinal Reformation in England" alongside justification *sola fide*.[14]

It is popular to describe the religious ethos in Reformation England as a middle way between Rome and Geneva. Classically, John Henry Newman claimed the Church of England adopted a *via media* between Protestantism and Popery.[15] The chief architect of the English Reformation, Archbishop Cranmer, "would violently have rejected such a notion: how could one have a middle way between truth and Antichrist?" Instead, what he sought was to be a 'reformed Catholic,' steering away from Popery and Anabaptism which he equally considered to be sects, but including Lutheranism as part of the Protestant middle ground.[16] Many sixteenth and seventeenth century Reformers and Reformed theologians wanted to be known not as Calvinists but as "Catholic Christians," conceiving of the Church of England as "Catholic and Reformed."[17] A. G.

---

[13] Moore, *English Hypothetical Universalism*, 227.

[14] M. L. Loane, *Masters of the English Reformation* (London: Church Bookroom Press, 1954), x.

[15] J. H. Newman, *Via Media of the Anglican Church* Volume 2 (London: B.M. Pickering, 1877), 33. For an effective historical refutation of more modern attempts see N. Tyacke, "Anglican Attitudes: some recent writings on English religious history, from the Reformation to the Civil War," in *Aspects of English Protestantism c. 1530-1700* (Manchester: Manchester University Press, 2001), 176-202 where he particularly interacts with key arguments for the doctrinal *via media* reading of early Anglicanism in Peter White, *Predestination, Policy and Polemic: Conflict and Consensus in the English Church from the Reformation to the Civil War* (Cambridge: Cambridge University Press, 1992).

[16] D. MacCulloch, *Thomas Cranmer: A Life* (London: Yale University Press, 1996), 617.

[17] See A. Milton, *Catholic and Reformed: The Roman and Protestant Churches in English Protestant Thought, 1600-1640* (Cambridge: Cambridge University Press, 2002), 407-408.

Dickens anachronistically attempts to see "The Origins of Anglicanism" (by which he means a blend of evangelical, catholic, and liberal theologies) in the ebb and flow of the Henrician church's struggles, all codified into the Settlement of 1559. But Cranmer himself would have rejected the notion of a Henrician *via media* defined this way, as all about "balance and comprehension rather than... a narrow orthodoxy."[18] With a free hand, unhindered by the whims of a vacillating monarch, the Primate of All England pursued a vigorous Reformed agenda in the years after 1547, which formed the basis for the continued success of the Reformed approach after the brief period of persecution under Mary.

Mary's propaganda campaign through pulpit and press was devastatingly effective for a time. Yet it was ultimately unsuccessful in erasing the gains already made by the Reformed. In her sister Elizabeth's reign, English Calvinists like William Perkins (1558-1602) had an international reputation and even the Archbishops of Canterbury at this time were all solidly Reformed in their outlook on predestination and other aspects of soteriology. The works of Calvin and other Swiss Reformers like Bullinger were held in very high regard in England. In 1586, for example, Archbishop Whitgift ordered that ministers should buy a Bible, a note book, and a copy of Bullinger's Reformed masterpiece, *The Decades*. They were to read a chapter of the Bible every day and make notes on it. Then every week they had to read a chapter of Bullinger too, and make notes on that. The notes were to be shown to someone regularly, and if they didn't prove acceptable the clergyman was to be censured.[19] Individual bishops could also set their clergy the task of reading and digesting other works such as Calvin's *Institutes* and Peter Martyr's *Commonplaces* which were, for example, the assigned reading in Norwich Diocese in 1589.[20]

Alongside the Bible in English, Foxe's *Acts and Monuments* (the "Book of Martyrs") and Bishop Jewel's *Apology of the Church of England*

---

[18] A. G. Dickens, *The English Reformation* 2nd ed. (London: B. T. Batsford, 1989), 205-206.

[19] See "Orders for the better increase of learning in the inferior ministers," in J. Strype, *The Life and Acts of John Whitgift D.D.* Volume 3 (Oxford: Clarendon Press, 1822), 194. Bullinger's *Fiftie Godlie and Learned Sermons* was published in English in 1577, and reprinted in 1587, no doubt in response to the Archbishop's directions.

[20] P. Hughes, *The Reformation in England III: 'True Religion Now Established'* (New York: Macmillan, 1954), 141.

were ordered to be placed in every parish church.[21] Later Roman Catholic and Laudian polemicists would attack Foxe and his heroes as "Zwinglians and Calvinists."[22] One Roman Catholic complained that "The Institutions of Calvin are so greatly esteemed in England, that the book has been most accurately translated into English, and is even fixed in the parish churches for people to read," while another lamented that "English bishops enjoin all the clergy to get the book almost by heart, never to have it out of their hands, to lay it by them in a conspicuous part of their pulpits."[23] The Geneva Bible (1560) with its outspoken and clearly Calvinist marginal notes was the Bible read and studied by every literate class of the population. Even opponents of this theology have noted its historical dominance. Hardwick confessed that Calvinist opinions "were predominant in almost every town and parish" in the Elizabethan years,[24] and Dickens speaks of the "immense influence" of Calvinism over the country at this time.[25] These are not signs of a church that thinks of itself as half way to Rome, and moving away from Geneva. The Established Church was Reformed — the 'narrow orthodoxy' of salvation by grace alone through faith alone was the creed of the English-speaking world.

2.2. *The Lutheran Link*

That is not to say that there were no other influences on the English Reformation up to the end of the sixteenth century. Doubtless there were some contrary, some confused, some moderate, and some indifferent clergy and laity in the ranks of the Protestant Reformed Church of England. "Everyone — well, almost everyone — talked and thought and cared about religion," writes Christopher Haigh, "But they did so with different levels of concentration and enthusiasm," and, we might add,

---

[21] See J. Strype, *Annals of the Reformation and Establishment of Religion* Volume 3 Part 1 (Oxford: Clarendon Press, 1824), 738.

[22] D. MacCulloch, *The Boy King: Edward VI and the Protestant Reformation* (California: University of California Press, 1999), 170-171; A. Milton, *Laudian and Royalist Polemic in Seventeenth-Century England: The Career and Writings of Peter Heylyn* (Manchester: Manchester University Press, 2007), 84, 201, 229.

[23] The complaints of Stapelton and Scultingius quoted in A. M. Toplady, *The Complete Works of Augustus Toplady* (Harrisburg, Virginia: Sprinkle Publications, 1987), 258. See 261 for Calvin's reputation in the universities and Milton, *Catholic and Reformed*, 396 for another assessment of Calvin's influence, from "an apostate."

[24] C. Hardwick, *A History of the Articles of Religion* (London: Bell and Daldy, 1859), 167.

[25] Dickens, *The English Reformation*, 205.

orthodoxy.[26] It would be foolish to pretend this was a golden age when everyone was Evangelical, Reformed, and deadly keen.

Apart from natural human diversity of temperament, however, some have seen in the English Reformation settlement, at the national level, a mixture of distinct Lutheran influences. This would be unsurprising at a stage when Lutheran-Reformed divides were only just opening up and an undifferentiated Protestant approach was discernible on many issues. The foundational documents of Anglican identity may naturally therefore bear some similarity in places to Lutheran texts. Nineteenth century commentators such as Richard Laurence in his 1804 Bampton Lectures go too far, however, when they assert that "the principles, upon which our Reformation was conducted, ought not to remain in doubt: they were manifestly Lutheran," and definitely not "Calvinistical."[27] According to Laurence and those of his school, the English Reformers "chose to give reputation to their opinions, and stability to their system, by adopting, where reason permitted, Lutheran sentiments, and expressing themselves in Lutheran language."[28]

There were delicate negotiations at one stage with the Lutherans, but these were abortive.[29] Cranmer produced what Gerald Bray calls "the most clearly Lutheran document ever to be penned by an English churchman," around this time (the so-called *Thirteen Articles* of 1538) but even then "Lutheran influence on Cranmer was far from being absolute," and this draft document never attained any official status.[30] The Lutheran-leaning interpretation conveniently overlooks Cranmer's developing

---

[26] C. A. Haigh, *The Plain Man's Pathways to Heaven: Kinds of Christianity in Post-Reformation England* (Oxford: Oxford University Press, 2007), 227.

[27] R. Laurence, *An Attempt to Illustrate those Articles of the Church of England which the Calvinists Improperly Consider as Calvinistical* (Oxford, 1820), 25.v.

[28] Laurence, *An Attempt to Illustrate those Articles*, 26. More specifically, on 15 and 45-46 Laurence claims the language was borrowed from the Confessions of Augsburg and "Wirtemberg" (*sic*), a point also made in the similarly anti-Calvinist reading of Hardwick, *A History of the Articles of Religion*, 127-128. Amongst more recent writers, R. Burrows, *John Wesley in the Reformation Tradition: The Protestant and Puritan Nature of Methodism Rediscovered* (Stoke-on-Trent: Tentmaker, 2009), 31 perpetuates this view of a Lutheran-Anglican link.

[29] See Hardwick, *A History of the Articles of Religion*, 52-66 on this.

[30] G. Bray, *Documents of the English Reformation* (Cambridge: James Clarke and Co., 1994), 184. The Thirteen Articles were only rediscovered at the beginning of the nineteenth century, which may account for Laurence and Hardwick's enthusiasm in pursuing their Lutheran reading of the Articles at around this time. Hardwick refers to the rediscovery in *A History of the Articles of Religion*, 60ff.

convictions on the main issue disputed between Lutherans and the Reformed. It is briefly glossed as merely being about "one single point,"[31] but Cranmer's view on the real presence of Christ in the Eucharist was decisive and determinative for the future direction of the English Reformation. It is doubtful that Cranmer ever held to the Lutheran doctrines of consubstantiation and the ubiquity of Christ's human nature, but by the reign of Edward VI it was clear that he had rejected them, as had others such as Latimer.[32] As MacCulloch has so effectively shown, 'Reformed' Christianity "effectively supplanted the Lutheran style within English Protestantism, and provided the dominant religious atmosphere in the Church of England until the death of James I. It was through Archbishop Cranmer himself that [this] distinct evangelical stance entered England."[33] We will return to the revisionist reading of Anglican origins which elevates the impact of continental Lutheranism later in the story.

A. G. Dickens avers that the English Reformation was one of "compromise and detachment, partly because these attitudes come naturally to the English temperament, partly in consequence of a patriotic distrust for foreign models."[34] Yet the Reformation here did not ignore such foreign pressures in an isolationist manner but rather religious leaders took sides in disputes between competing theologies from Europe, adopting some and firmly rejecting others. The ramifications of the doctrinal paradigm shift in favour of the Reformed were far-reaching, especially after Bucer and Vermigli — leading *non-Lutheran* Reformers from the continent — were given prominent theological professorships and influence over Prayer Book revision in Edward VI's reign. The Reformed, as opposed to Lutheran, stream of the Reformation gave somewhat greater prominence to God's sovereignty, the covenant motif, the role of community in Christian faith over the more individualistic emphasis of Luther, and had a greater interest in good works (evidenced in its less radical separation of law and gospel, and the development of the

[31] "The opinions therefore of the Primate were at this time perfectly Lutheran; and although he afterwards changed them in one single point, in other respects they remained unaltered." Laurence, *An Attempt to Illustrate those Articles*, 17. Cf. 41.

[32] See J. I. Packer, "Thomas Cranmer's Catholic Theology," in *Honouring the People of God: Collected Shorter Works of J. I. Packer Volume 4* (Carlisle: Paternoster, 1999), 242-243.

[33] MacCulloch, *Thomas Cranmer*, 173.

[34] Dickens, *The English Reformation*, 206.

'third use' of the Law).[35] These emphases and influences are discernable in many of the English Reformers and are certainly present in the foundational documents of Anglican theology.[36] To summarise, in the words of Gerald Bray and Paul Gardner,

> the Church of England never became 'Lutheran' in any recognisable sense, and there have been times since the sixteenth century when theological relations between the two communions have been less than cordial. This is at least partly because Anglicans have taken their theological framework not from Lutheranism, but from the Reformed churches, whose covenant theology was mediated to them by a long succession of divines... there is no doubt that Anglican theology has moved in the orbit of Reformed theology, rather than of Lutheran, for most of its post-Reformation history.[37]

So while Luther was undoubtedly a huge influence on the English Reformation, he had no monopoly of influence over the Reformers or the constitution of the Church of England, which drew decisive inspiration from the other major stream of continental Protestantism. The doctrine of the Evangelical Reformers, as John Owen helpfully summarised it some time later, "was the same with that of the churches abroad called particularly Reformed, in distinction from the Lutherans."[38] It is possible to go back even further, however, and find the source and inspiration for the Church of England's doctrine not in Luther or Calvin but in Augustine. As Wylie put it, "As regards the doctrine of the Articles, all those divines who have been the more thoroughly versed in theology, both in its history and in its substance... have acknowledged that, in the main, the Articles follow in the path of the great doctor of the West,

---

[35] See the summary in C. R. Trueman, *Luther's Legacy: Salvation and English Reformers 1525-1556* (Oxford: Clarendon Press, 1994), 75-80. Trueman examines Reformed influence in Tyndale, Frith, Barnes, Hooper, and Bradford.

[36] For Anglican approaches to the Law, for example, see the use of the Ten Commandments in the 1662 Communion Service, and Article 7 on the Old Testament Law.

[37] G. Bray and P. Gardner, "The Joint Declaration on the Doctrine of Justification," *Churchman* 115/2 (2001), 112.

[38] *An Inquiry into the Original, Nature, Institution, Power, Order, and Commission of Evangelical Churches* in W. H. Goold (ed.), *The Works of John Owen* (Edinburgh: Hunter and Johnstone, 1850-1853), 15:207.

Augustine."[39] We will also return to this link later in the narrative.

2.3. *Uneasy with the Reformation*

For a time, the reforming party in the English Church was simply known by the undifferentiated name of 'Evangelical.' However, Evangelicals were not alone in seeking to influence the direction of the establishment. J. H. Merle d'Aubigné identifies two anti-papist factions in the Church of England in 1536: "the evangelicals and the Anglican Catholics who were halting between the two extremes" of Protestantism and Rome.[40] The continued presence of a more 'Catholic' element within the establishment at this stage cannot be denied, and the Elizabethan Settlement held out some small compromises to such clergy in the hope of winning their allegiance. Yet the more 'high church' faction did not dominate the mainstream, realising that it was somewhat out on a limb in its lack of comfort within the Reformed establishment. In the mid-nineteenth century, John Henry Newman challenged even the Protestant nature of the Thirty-nine Articles, in his infamous Tract XC, but for the Anglican Catholics of the Elizabethan age such grand claims were almost unthinkable and they sought instead to subvert the settlement or to work within its bounds, especially when anti-Roman Catholic sentiment was at its height.

The Anglican Catholic group was not alone in its discomfort with Queen Elizabeth's determined resolution to stand still religiously after 1559. The Reformed Church of England was agreed in one important principle with the Lutherans, that of the so-called normative principle: the English Reformation was generally conducted along the lines that whatever is not prohibited in Scripture is permitted, as long as it is agreeable to the peace and unity of the Church. The Church of England, for example, therefore retained bishops whereas the Reformed on the continent (following the *regulative* principle, that whatever is not commanded is prohibited) generally abandoned episcopacy in favour of Presbyterianism. Not everyone was in agreement with this way of settling matters: the puritans of the late sixteenth century continued to seek

[39] J. A. Wylie, *The History of Protestantism: Volume 4* (Rapidan, VA: Hartland, 2002), 1867.

[40] J. H. Merle d'Aubigné, *The Reformation in England: Volume 2* (Edinburgh: Banner of Truth, 1963), 353. See the similar taxonomy in Hardwick, *A History of the Articles of Religion*, 31.

further reformation of church government and the abolition of various practices which they considered to be a hangover from the medieval past, such as the sign of the cross used in baptism or the use of the surplice and other vestments.

The puritans have been criticised for operating a church within the Church. As Patrick Collinson remarked, puritans within the established church often "conducted themselves sometimes like separatists, sometimes like tenacious if aggrieved members of the establishment, and the discomfort of this ambiguous position was virtually chronic."[41] They remained within the fabric of the Church of England and pressed for further reform through preaching, politics, publishing, and conferences which some claimed were the skeletal framework for a parallel Presbyterianism within the episcopal system. Many were happy with, or at least tolerant of, episcopal government when it was exercised by godly men who allowed puritan ministry to flourish, while others exhibited what Collinson describes as "incipient congregationalism," or "the free church spirit."[42] As their hopes for parish reformations were frustrated, they increasingly formed cells within communities or networked and gathered across parish boundaries in non-parochial settings, using forms of service and concepts of church governance imported from churches abroad.

Yet these nonconformists were almost always Reformed in their wider theological commitments. They shared a common approach to soteriology and sacramentology with the establishment, even while they pursued a more progressive ecclesiology. Archbishop Grindal incurred the wrath of the Queen with his support for the puritan practice of "prophesyings," clergy meetings for the practice and improvement of preaching — a very puritan concern. Archbishop Whitgift, on the other hand, would proactively seek to stamp out nonconformity, loyal to the forms but not perhaps the spirit of the Edwardian Reformation.[43] Yet both Grindal and Whitgift were staunchly Reformed in their doctrinal convictions, and so such clashes were less fraught than they would become in the next century with the rise of an *avant-garde* theology allied to the old ceremonial.

---

[41] P. Collinson, *The Elizabethan Puritan Movement* (Oxford: Clarendon Press, 1967), 132-133.

[42] Collinson, *The Elizabethan Puritan Movement*, 333.

[43] See the comments in MacCulloch, *The Boy King*, 194.

Richard Hooker (1554-1600) is often seen as the theologian of the *via media* (between Geneva and Rome) thanks in part to the revisionist efforts of the Oxford Movement in the nineteenth century. Yet properly set in his own context, Hooker can also be seen as standing within this mainstream of sixteenth century Reformed orthodoxy. As Nigel Atkinson has shown, though he opposed some extreme puritan and Presbyterian views, "Hooker, and the Church of England, embraced the Reformation and in fact willingly adopted a Reformed position in all cardinal doctrinal tenets."[44]

2.4. *The Arminian Challenge*

Dutch theologian, Jakob Harmenszoon was born in 1560 and ordained in 1588 after studying under Beza in Geneva. A Professor at Leiden, he Latinized his name as "Arminius." Interestingly, this may have been a way of linking himself with another man, more famous at that time, a German tribal chieftain called Arminius who opposed the Roman Empire at the start of the 1st century AD.[45] That Arminius was used during the Reformation as a symbol of the 'German' people and their fight against Rome.[46] Yet many saw in this new Arminius and his theology a slippery slope that would lead Reformed Christians straight back into the arms of the Pope.

Some ideas which were later to be famously associated with the name of Arminius were being debated in Cambridge at the end of the 16th century. William Barrett, a fellow of Caius College preached a virulent sermon against Calvin, Beza, Peter Martyr Vermigli, and Zanchius for their doctrine of election.[47] In response to this challenge the Regius Professor of Divinity, Dr. Whitaker, produced what are known as the Lambeth Articles. These nine brief statements of Reformed thought on

---

[44] N. Atkinson, *Richard Hooker and the Authority of Scripture, Tradition and Reason: Reformed Theologian of the Church of England?* (Vancouver, BC: Regent College Publishing, 2005), xv, building on the work of W. J. Torrance Kirby, *Richard Hooker's Doctrine of the Royal Supremacy* (Leiden: E. J. Brill, 1990).

[45] R. Lane Fox, *The Classical World: An Epic History of Greece and Rome* (London: Penguin, 2006), 477.

[46] See W. Bradford Smith, "German Pagan Antiquity in Lutheran Historical Thought," *The Journal of the Historical Society* 4.3 (2004), 357-358, and 372 n.28 on Harmenszoon's fellow countryman Erasmus as the new Arminius leading the fight against Roman tyranny.

[47] P. Schaff, *The Creeds of Christendom. Volume 3: The Evangelical Protestant Creeds* (Grand Rapids: Baker, 1996 [1876]), 659.

predestination and perseverance were intended to clarify the meaning of the Thirty-nine Articles and vindicate their Reformed credentials.[48] They were approved by Archbishop Whitgift and Archbishop Hutton of York, and a number of others who met at Lambeth Palace in November 1595. The Queen was unhappy that these men had met 'in synod' without her express permission, and so the Lambeth Articles were never given royal approval. Yet they clearly demonstrate the nature of the prevailing orthodoxy at the time.

Arminian doctrine, described by one historian as "an elastic, progressive, changing liberalism,"[49] spread rapidly in the Netherlands. After the death of Arminius in 1609, forty-six of his followers there issued a 'Remonstrance' or protest against the Calvinist orthodoxy of the great majority of their fellow ministers.[50] They summarised their creed under five points, including conditional predestination (God only chooses people he foresees will have faith), universal atonement (Christ's death obtained salvation for everyone without exception, making them saveable, though none enjoy forgiveness until they believe), and the idea that our wills can resist God's, concerning our salvation and perseverance. A counter-remonstrance was issued by Calvinists and a conference was held in 1611 between the two parties but with no agreement reached.[51] Then in 1618 after much controversy and preparation, the Synod of Dort was convened to respond to the Arminian five points.[52] As Schaff notes, this was "the only Synod of a quasi-œcumenical character in the history of the Reformed Churches" since delegates from the Reformed churches of

[48] For the text of the Lambeth Articles in Latin and English see P. Schaff, *The Creeds of Christendom. Volume 3*, 523-524. For Richard Hooker's summary and slight modification of these Articles, again reiterating his Reformed view of predestination, see the end of Book V, Appendix 1 in R. Hooker, *Of the Laws of Ecclesiastical Polity (Book V)* Everyman's Library No. 202 (London: J. M. Dent and Sons, 1907), 542-543.

[49] P. Schaff, *The Creeds of Christendom. Volume 1: The History of Creeds* (Grand Rapids: Baker, 1996 [1876]), 509.

[50] For the text see Schaff, *The Creeds of Christendom: Volume 3*, 545-549.

[51] For the history of the controversy, see L. Praamsma, "The Background of the Arminian Controversy (1586-1618)," in P. Y. De Jong (ed.), *Crisis in the Reformed Churches: Essays in Commemoration of the Great Synod of Dort 1618-1619* (Grandville, MI: Reformed Fellowship, 2008), 39-56.

[52] Note that the famous "Five Points of Calvinism" were therefore framed in a polemical content against the original "Five Points of Arminianism." They were not discussed in the order which the later mnemonic TULIP would suggest (Total depravity, Unconditional election, Limited atonement, Irresistible grace, Preservation of the saints), although this can be a helpful memory aid and seems peculiarly appropriate when summarising the conclusions of a meeting in Holland.

several other countries were invited to attend with voting rights.[53] A delegation was requested and sent from Britain by King James I, himself a Calvinist. This was not uncontroversial; as Anthony Milton points out, it provoked "an ecclesiastical counterpart to the political debates of our age over how far Britain should be considered as part of the European community."[54] Indeed, as he continues,

> The presence of the English divines at perhaps the most important Reformed synod to meet before modern times has often raised eyebrows and temperatures in the Church of England, provoking constant and sometimes agonized debate among Anglican scholars and church historians ever since. It has, perhaps inevitably, become a significant issue in the perennial debates about how close the Church of England should consider itself to continental Protestantism, and one that is perhaps all the more striking in that the synod occurred, not in the early stages of England's Reformation, but several generations further on, when any 'Anglican' identity might have been assumed to have come to full fruition.[55]

Although some have dismissed British involvement at Dort as a temporary foreign-policy manoeuvre, it does seem that the essentially Reformed doctrinal identity of the Church of England was, at the time, widely recognised internationally even if it was hotly disputed by later Laudian polemicists.[56] It is no surprise then that this has been ignored or passed over in recent discussions of Anglican identity.[57] Yet other historians are now beginning to recognise that Englishmen played a leading role as part of a 'Calvinist internationalism' in this period, such

---

[53] Schaff, *The Creeds of Christendom: Volume 1*, 514.

[54] A. Milton (ed.), *The British Delegation and the Synod of Dort (1618-1619)* Church of England Record Society Volume 13 (Woodbridge, Suffolk: The Boydell Press, 2005), xxii.

[55] Milton, *The British Delegation and the Synod of Dort*, xviii.

[56] See P. Heylyn, *Historia Quinqu-Articularis: or, a Declaration of the Judgement of the Western Churches; and more particularly the Church of England in the Five Controverted Points; Reproached in these last times by the name of Arminianism* (London, 1660) which was answered by a defence of the Anglican credentials of the five points from H. Hickman, *Historia Quinq-Articularis Exarticulata; or Animadversions on Dr. Heylin's Quinquarticular History in which... The Doctrine of the Arminians, in the five points, is proved, to be contrary to the Doctrine of the Reformed Church of England* (1673).

[57] See Milton, *The British Delegation and the Synod of Dort*, xx-xxi as well as Tyacke, "Anglican Attitudes," 186 and his "Puritanism, Arminianism and counter-revolution," in the same volume, 140.

that a distinctive Reformed theological sympathy transcended national boundaries and motivated even our military involvement in Europe[58].

Moreover, as Nicholas Tyacke has repeatedly demonstrated, "until the 1620s Calvinists generally controlled the English licensing of religious books, under the aegis of [the bishops of] Canterbury and London in the capital, and the determination of orthodoxy in university disputations."[59] In the wake of the Gunpowder Plot (1605), the Calvinist puritans benefited from the redirection of the government's energies away from nonconformist Protestants towards countering Roman Catholicism.[60] At this point, with the majority of the clergy and educated laity doctrinally committed to Reformed doctrine, the Reformed consensus seemed almost unassailable, until "a doctrinal revolution took place within the established church which shattered the Jacobean dispensation... during the 1620s the Calvinist heritage was overthrown and with it the prerequisite of English Protestant unity."[61]

The rise of Arminianism under Archbishop Laud was to prove the most divisive factor in English religious and political life during the seventeenth century. English Arminianism was often accompanied by royalism, sacramentalism, and sacerdotalism with an emphasis on monarchy, priesthood, episcopacy, altar, and church decoration in a way that Dutch Arminianism (a Presbyterian, republican, and separatist phenomenon) did not envisage.[62] This led many to the conclusion that it was simply a means to an end — the overturning of the Reformation and the re-introduction of Roman Catholicism. Richard Montagu, a well-known Arminian, and even Archbishop Laud himself were indeed involved in discussions over possible reconciliation schemes with Rome,[63] and Laud banned the publication of all books identifying the papacy as Antichrist.[64] The Catholic alliances of Charles I (who married Henrietta Maria of France in 1625 after a failed plan to marry Maria Anna of Spain,

---

[58] See D. Trim, "Calvinist Internationalism and the English Officer Corps, 1562–1642," *History Compass* 4/6 (2006), 1024–1048.

[59] "Anglican Attitudes," 179.

[60] In "Puritanism, Arminianism and counter-revolution," 137 Tyacke points out that "from 1611 until 1618 no work directed specifically against Puritanism, either in its nonconformist or Presbyterian guises, is recorded in the Stationers' Registers as being licensed for the press."

[61] Tyacke, "Puritanism, Arminianism and counter-revolution," 141.

[62] See Milton, *Catholic and Reformed*, 438.

[63] See Milton, *Laudian and Royalist Polemic*, 97, 208-9.

[64] Milton, *Catholic and Reformed*, 120.

future Holy Roman Empress) lent further credence to this idea.

There were many allegations of a conspiracy between Arminians and Rome. The Cardinal of Lorraine was said to have paid an annual salary to several German Lutheran professors to write against Calvinists, since it was conducive to the Roman Catholic cause to encourage Arminianism and sow dissension amongst the Protestants.[65] An English Jesuit's letter to his superior in Brussels dated March 1628 (allegedly found amongst Archbishop Laud's papers) also reported, "We have planted that soveraigne drugge Arminianisme, which we hope will purge the Protestants from their heresie."[66] Hence it is no surprise that Arminian theology was portrayed, even by moderate opponents, as a revival of Pelagianism (an ancient heresy denying original sin and the absolute need for grace), and a slippery slope back to Rome.[67]

Yet the Laudian agenda was more positively presented by its most prominent propagandist Peter Heylyn as the rediscovery of the original foundations of the Reformation. Over time Heylyn developed patterns of defence for the new theology and ecclesiastical style which would be used well into the future. One popular Arminian ploy (borrowed from Romanist polemics) was to intimate that Reformed theology was an insidiously 'foreign' influence, emanating particularly from Switzerland but also from the foreign wives of men like Cranmer, Hooper, and Coverdalc.[68] Yet in an attempt to distance the Church of England from Calvinism, Heylyn enthusiastically linked Laudianism to Melanchthonian Lutheranism.

Heylyn made this link for several reasons.[69] First, the Lutherans had retained images in churches as well as 'Popish' apparel which was popular with the Laudians, while remaining firmly Protestant. Second, post-Luther Lutheranism owed more to Luther's successor, Philip

---

[65] See John Owen, *A Display of Arminianism: Being a Discovery of the Old Pelagian Idol, Free Will, with the New Goddess Contingency, Advancing Themselves into the Throne of the God of Heaven, to the Prejudice of his Grace in The Works of John Owen*, 10:7.

[66] See Toplady, *Complete Works*, 55. Toplady's source for this is William Prynne, *Hidden workes of darkenes brought to publike light* (1645) but it should be noted that Prynne was not always a very reliable source.

[67] See Milton, *Catholic and Reformed*, 418.

[68] See MacCulloch, *The Boy King*, 167, 170-172. See also his, *Reformation: Europe's House Divided 1490-1700* (London: Penguin, 2004), 510.

[69] See Milton, *Laudian and Royalist Polemic*, 179, 231-232 on this novel development in Heylyn's thought. Milton, *Catholic and Reformed*, 444 also mentions extreme Anti-Calvinist pamphleteer Thomas Pierce who makes the same links.

Melanchthon, on the topics of free will and predestination than to Luther's own 'Calvinism *avant la lettre*' as seen in his great exchange with Erasmus in *The Bondage of the Will*.[70] Melanchthon's early work, the *Loci Communes* (1521), shows certain affinities at points with the common Protestant thrust of the Thirty-nine Articles,[71] but later in his career Melanchthon changed his mind, moving away from and undermining Luther's Reformational theology.[72] Third, there was polemical distance between the German Lutherans and the Reformed due particularly to their inability to agree on the Lord's Supper, but also political and military distance (for reasons we need not go into here).[73]

For these reasons, a link between later Lutheranism and Arminianism was often embraced by polemicists such as Heylyn. As Tyacke rightly concludes, "English and Dutch anti-Calvinists shared a common ancestor in second-generation Lutheranism."[74] These links had been noted by English Calvinists in the 1590s who dubbed their opponents 'Lutherans,'[75] but the connections were enthusiastically emphasised later by Heylyn as a way of portraying international Calvinism as usurping the true spirit of the Reformation in 'the Anglican church.'[76]

In the nineteenth century, Richard Laurence, who shared Heylyn's general perspective on these matters, implied that because Calvinists tried to add to the Thirty-nine Articles by means of the Lambeth Articles or amend them in the Westminster Assembly, they obviously knew the original Articles were not Calvinist.[77] The Westminster divines'

---

[70] On which see L. Gatiss, "The Manifesto of the Reformation: Luther vs. Erasmus on Free Will," *Churchman* 123/3 (2009), 203-225.

[71] See *Loci Communes Theologici* trans. L. J. Satre, rev. W. Pauck in W. Pauck (ed.), *Melanchthon and Bucer* (London: Westminster John Knox Press, 1969), 18-152.

[72] See Trueman, *Luther's Legacy*, 74.

[73] See e.g. Milton, *Catholic and Reformed*, 388 for more details.

[74] Tyacke, "Anglican Attitudes," 179. See also 178, 181 and 196 as well as his "Puritanism, Arminianism and counter-revolution," 142 and "Defining Arminianism," in the same volume, 156-157.

[75] See Milton, *Catholic and Reformed*, 386-388.

[76] He was one of the first to use the term "Anglican church," in his *Ecclesias Restaurata* ed. J. C. Robertson (Cambridge, 1849; 1661 edn), I, 193. The term "Anglianism", a variant of "Anglicanism", first appears in print in Thomas Harrab's Roman Catholic polemic, *Tessaradelphus* (1616), which says, "I call the religion of England Anglianism, because it among the rest hath no one especial author, but is set forth by the Prince and Parliament."

[77] Laurence, *An Attempt to Illustrate those Articles*, 194-195.

work on the Articles arose out of their commission from Parliament "to free and vindicate the Doctrine of them from all aspersions and false interpretations." They were limited "onely to the clearing and vindicating of them," and probably made fewer alterations than they would have liked to had they been given a freer hand.[78] So their intention was merely to clarify ambiguities and exclude false interpretations of the Articles, not to superimpose entirely novel doctrines onto the text. Their efforts ceased because Parliament ordered them to direct their efforts elsewhere and not, as Laurence supposes, because they found the task impossible. Indeed, it is impressive how little they altered as they very effectively glossed the Articles in one or two places in the light of a century of intense theological controversy.[79]

Ultimately, the rather obnoxious and ambitious Archbishop Laud succeeded, alongside a king with a taste for absolutist rule, in uniting everyone who disliked him. So it was no surprise when during the ensuing civil wars, which had religious issues right at their heart, Laud had his head removed on Tower Hill in January 1645. Charles I's head joined it in 1649, thus beginning the period known as the Commonwealth or Interregnum.[80] During 1649-1660 a widespread Reformed consensus prevailed throughout Great Britain. Certainly there was great religious freedom in the republic and under Cromwell; all kinds of nutcases had liberty to indulge in their weird and wacky beliefs and to publish their rantings and ravings without censorship. Yet with men like John Owen training pastors at Oxford, and the Westminster Assembly writing its Confession and Catechisms and screening appointments to churches, it was clear in which direction things were facing. Men with different theological persuasions within a broadly Reformed umbrella were tolerated by the Commonwealth establishment, while disagreements over secondary issues such as infralapsarianism or infant baptism were

---

[78] *The Proceedings of the Assembly of Divines upon the Thirty nine Articles of the Church of England* (London, 1646), 1-2. The revision of the Articles was undertaken in 1643 but not presented to Parliament until later.

[79] Most obviously they re-worked Article 3 on Christ's descent into hell to make it less ambiguous, and somewhat expanded Article 11 on justification. Their slight adjustment in the language of Article 10 on free will did not make it any more obnoxious to an Erasmian doctrine of 'free will' than it already was, and arguably restored an emphasis that had been lost when Cranmer's Article 10 "Of Grace" from the Forty-two Articles of 1553 was dropped as part of the reduction in the number of Articles.

[80] Anglican ministers should note that not every interregnum needs to begin with a beheading!

kept in perspective.[81] As John Spurr has written, "The result was a decentralized church with great clerical discretion and local variety, still supported by tithes. Among the parish clergy were Presbyterians, Independents, a handful of Baptists, and a significant number of individuals who can best be described as 'prayer-book men' or former episcopalians or even 'Anglicans.'"[82]

Arminianism allied to Catholicism and the arbitrary abuse of royal power had been overturned. Reformed theology was once again back on top, albeit now with something of a Presbyterian and puritan flavour rather than an Anglican one. Great Britain was united, the Scots (always more open to Calvinist influence) strengthening the Reformed tendency through the Solemn League and Covenant as well as their significant involvement at the Westminster Assembly. Yet this was not to last.

2.5. *The Arminian Supremacy*

Without a king, England failed to achieve sufficient political stability. Too much rested on Cromwell and the military while the puritan agenda taken to excess in some areas failed to win hearts and minds. Parliament called for the return of Charles I's son as king. Charles II promised his subjects that on his return there would be a "liberty for tender consciences and that no man shall be ... called in question for differences of opinion in matters of religion which do not disturb the peace of the kingdom."[83] This was greeted with delighted optimism. Richard Baxter and other leading puritan divines were appointed chaplains to the king and granted an audience with him. Nevertheless, all was not as it appeared behind the scenes. Perhaps the king himself was sincere enough in his statements but he was surrounded by men who were thirsting for revenge. Once he was safely back on the throne, Charles found that he had to make concessions to these Laudian extremists, and his good intentions were seriously compromised.

Arminianism flooded back into the country, allied to another king

---

[81] See L. Gatiss, *From Life's First Cry: John Owen on Infant Baptism and Infant Salvation* (London: Latimer Trust, 2008), 1-3, 39n87 for the influence of John Tombes, a prominent Anglican Anti-Paedobaptist, during the 1640s and 1650s.

[82] J. Spurr, *English Puritanism 1603-1689* (Basingstoke: Palgrave Macmillan, 1998), 118-119.

[83] *Declaration of King Charles II from Breda from G. Gould, Documents Relating to the Settlement of the Church of England by the Act of Uniformity of 1662* (London: W. Kent and Co, 1862), 3.

with a taste for arbitrary rule and another Roman Catholic Princess as a wife. His advisors and bishops proceeded quietly and cautiously to recapture the establishment by stealth. So while "the King might speak graciously to his Presbyterian subjects... his favour was showered on the Laudians."[84] In jostling for position at the Restoration, the Reformed of various persuasions (Anglican, Presbyterian, Independent) were divided and conquered. After some initial manoeuvring, a large contingent of Reformed ministers (and others) were ejected from the Church of England between 1660-1663, and both they and the constituency which they represented then suffered a period of persecution and suppression.[85]

The 'Glorious Revolution' and the Act of Toleration of 1689 brought respite from the bitterness of these years, and saw the establishment of legal dissent. Conformity and nonconformity, rather than being parties vying for influence within the same established church, became the separate institutions we know today as the Church of England and the 'Free Churches.' As Carl Trueman has written, 'The Great Ejection of 1662 effectively removed from the Church, and thus from the intellectual establishment, the vast majority of those ministers committed to a more thoroughly Reformed faith; it therefore surrendered both the Church, and, as a result, the academy to a group whose theological concerns were generally more latitudinarian. '[86]

There were also theological problems within the dissenting community. A stress on 'the Bible alone' to the exclusion of systematic and historical theology led to a great many Presbyterian, Congregational, and Baptist churches being fatally infected with Unitarianism in the century after the Great Ejection. As Watts says, "their neo-Arminianism predisposed them to look more favourably than their Calvinist brethren on liberal trends in theology."[87] This was due in no small part to greatly weakened (sometimes resolutely non-existent) ministerial subscription to articles of faith. The drift towards Arianism or Socinianism was evident within the Church of England to some extent also, but many within the

---

[84] R. S. Bosher, *The Making of the Restoration Settlement: The Influence of the Laudians 1649-1662* (London: Dacre Press, 1951), 155.

[85] See L. Gatiss, *The Tragedy of 1662: The Ejection and Persecution of the Puritans* (London: Latimer Trust, 2007).

[86] C. Trueman, *The Claims of Truth: John Owen's Trinitarian Theology* (Carlisle: Paternoster, 1998), 2.

[87] See M. Watts, *The Dissenters: From the Reformation to the French Revolution* (Oxford: Clarendon Press, 1978), 376.

bounds of the national church retained a great sympathy for Reformed theology, which would later prove to be a force for the church's renewal and revival.

Some historians speak of the post-Restoration eclipse or "overthrow of Calvinism."[88] J. I. Packer says that after the Restoration, "Calvinism had the status only of an oddity maintained by nonconformists."[89] Yet as Stephen Hampton has recently demonstrated, after 1662 the Reformed may not have been in the majority but they remained nonetheless, an extremely significant group within the Church.[90] Conscious of standing within a much wider European Reformed tradition, they were also keen to demonstrate that they were the heirs of a respectable home-grown branch of that movement. Many of these men taught what Hampton calls "Reformed divinity, but with Restoration curlicues,"[91] that is, ornamental twists associated with the neo-Laudian agenda such as a devotion to episcopacy as of the *esse* of the church, the suppression of nonconformity, and High Church stage props like robes, candles, elaborate church architecture and furnishings.[92] This makes the Reformed Anglicanism of this period a somewhat peculiar and eccentric phenomenon within the wider intellectual movement, but still recognisably Reformed in terms of its soteriology and other major doctrinal commitments.

Too often when writing about the Evangelical Revival of the eighteenth century, writers have ignored the vibrancy of the conforming Reformed tradition in the latter half of the seventeenth century. J. C. Ryle for instance tells us that before the Evangelical Revival everything was natural theology, cold moral essays in the pulpit, nothing of the weighty Reformation doctrines for which our martyred reformers had gone to the stake, and sermons "utterly devoid of anything likely to awaken, convert, or save souls."[93] G. R. Balleine calls this "the Glacial Epoch in our Church

---

[88] G. R. Cragg, *From Puritanism to the Age of Reason: A Study of Changes in Religious Thought within the Church of England 1660 to 1700* (Cambridge: Cambridge University Press, 1966), 13-36.

[89] J. I. Packer, "Arminianisms," in *Honouring the People of God,* 289.

[90] S. Hampton, *Anti-Arminians: The Anglican Reformed Tradition from Charles II to George I* (Oxford: Oxford University Press, 2008), 269.

[91] Hampton, *Anti-Arminians,* 23.

[92] See Tyacke, "Arminianism and the theology of the Restoration Church," in *Aspects of English Protestantism,* 334 and Hampton, *Anti-Arminians,* 24.

[93] J. C. Ryle, *Christian Leaders of the Eighteenth Century* (Edinburgh: Banner of Truth, 1978 [1885]), 14.

History... only the cautious and the colourless remained... [with] a dreary, drab-coloured faith, devoid of power or beauty."[94]

This may not have been the age of passionately Reformed evangelistic giants, but it is incorrect to say as David Bebbington does that "the doctrine of justification by faith had well-nigh disappeared," and that there is scant evidence of a link between the Reformed tradition of the seventeenth century and the Evangelicals of the eighteenth.[95] Hampton identifies at least twelve bishops, six deans, and several senior divinity professors with decidedly Reformed credentials in this period, not to mention several of the greatest scientific minds, one of the most celebrated preachers, two eminent Patristic scholars, and some influential ecclesiastical courtiers.[96] Regarding the Reformed accounts of election and justification at this time, no less a Calvinist than John Owen claimed in 1674 that it was "maintained by the most learned of the dignified clergy at this day."[97] Such men worked hard to fortify a Reformed reading of the Thirty-nine Articles and the Prayer Book especially on justification, the Trinity, and predestination; and in Convocation they fiercely resisted the latitudinarian liberalism of bishops like Gilbert Burnet who sought to legitimate Arminianism with studiously ambiguous readings of the Articles.[98] This is hardly indicative of an invisible minority; indeed, it could well provoke Reformed Anglicans of the early twenty-first century to jealousy, languishing as they do without anything approaching this level of influence in the Church of England today.

2.6. *Summary*

In brief then, after the break with Rome under Henry VIII a native English Reformed tradition was firmly established in the reign of Edward VI under Archbishop Cranmer. This survived the persecutions of Mary and remained supreme, if somewhat frustrated in some quarters, under Elizabeth. Connections to the wider continental Reformed tradition were cherished and nurtured until these were brought under suspicion in the

[94] G. R. Balleine, *A History of the Evangelical Party in the Church of England* (London: Longmans, Green and Co., 1911), 10-11.

[95] D. W. Bebbington, *Evangelicalism in Modern Britain: A history from the 1730s to the 1980s* (London: Routledge, 1989), 36.

[96] Hampton, *Anti-Arminians*, 22.

[97] *A Vindication of Some Passages in a Discourse Concerning Communion with God in The Works of John Owen*, 2:304.

[98] Hampton, *Anti-Arminians*, 28-31.

early seventeenth century by Laudian revisionists seeking to draw the Church of England away from international Calvinism and to link it more closely with Rome and second-generation Lutheranism. Arminianism was again placed on the back foot by Parliamentary victory in the civil wars, but for various social and political reasons managed to emerge from the Commonwealth with the reigns of power once again firmly in hand. The Reformed community was outmanoeuvred and fragmented by the ejection of 1662, though a conforming remnant was able to retain significant strength within the established church despite the supremacy of Arminianism.

At the end of this turbulent period of our history, in 1689, the Coronation Oath for King William and Queen Mary was specifically written to bind the new monarchs to the established religion of their kingdoms. What did Scottish Presbyterians with their Westminster Confession have in common with their Episcopal English neighbours and their Thirty-nine Articles? Like the Dutch Calvinism of the new king, both were, in essence, considered different manifestations of "the true profession of the gospel... the Protestant Reformed religion." Kings had sworn to uphold the "true profession of the gospel" before, but only now was this more carefully defined. In the parliamentary debate about the Coronation Oath, it was initially suggested that the king be asked to maintain "the Protestant religion" only, without the additional qualifier. Perhaps some at this stage may have used "Reformed" merely as a synonym for non-Catholic, yet there was a recognition in the debate that there might be other forms of Protestant religion besides "Reformed," and that the (Lutheran) Augsburg Confession did not correspond as closely to it as might be imagined. It also seems to have been presupposed that adding "Reformed" narrowed the doctrinal emphasis while still denoting a doctrinal stance which could have varying manifestations in terms of church discipline, polity, and practice. Some Anabaptists called themselves "Reformed" too, MPs noted, and provided they demonstrate this by signing up to the doctrinal parts of the Thirty-nine Articles, their meetings were soon to be granted toleration.[99]

The Reformed faith had triumphed at the Reformation and despite its varying fortunes in the next few generations, it ultimately emerged as the official religion upon which the United Kingdom is founded.

---

[99] See A. Grey, *Debates of the House of Commons, from the year 1667 to the year 1694: Volume 9* (London, 1763), 190-198.

3. Reformed Theology in the Evangelical Revival

The easiest way to spot a heretic, a charlatan or a theological scoundrel is to know what such a person looks like, and church history is like one giant book of theologically criminal mug shots.

- Carl Trueman, "The Theological Importance of Criminal Profiling" http://solapanel.org (2009)

Study of the eighteenth century revivals has been dominated in recent years by the approach of David Bebbington's influential *Evangelicalism in Modern Britain*. In what has become a classic work, Bebbington outlines the distinctives of what he regards as a self-consciously unitary movement beginning in the 1730s. The special marks of Evangelical religion are, he says, "*conversionism*, the belief that lives need to be changed; *activism*, the expression of the gospel in effort; *biblicism*, a particular regard for the Bible; and what may be called *crucicentrism*, a stress on the sacrifice of Christ on the cross."[100]

Defining a movement is never a simple task, and it would be easy to criticise this 'quadrilateral' for being too imprecise and bland: could not a Roman Catholic, for example, also claim to be concerned with changing lives, expressing the gospel in action, having a regard for the Bible, and looking to the cross? In 1769, for example, Roman Catholic missionaries from Spain established the first of twenty-one missions in California with just such motives. Yet even if we treat Bebbington's imprecision more charitably, all of these Evangelical distinctives, as Carl Trueman and others have rightly pointed out, are deeply rooted in the Reformation and were certainly a part of Puritan religion well before Evangelicalism was supposedly 'created' by the Enlightenment.[101]

As we have already noted in the previous chapter, the reforming and Reformed party within the Church of England was known from early

---

[100] D. W. Bebbington, *Evangelicalism in Modern Britain: A history from the 1730s to the 1980s* (London: Routledge, 1989), 3.

[101] C. R. Trueman, "Reformers, Puritans and Evangelicals: The Lay Connection," in D. Lovegrove (ed.), *The Rise of the Laity in Evangelical Protestantism* (London: Routledge, 2002), 31-32. For further in-depth critiques of the Bebbington proposals see M. A. G. Haykin and K. J. Stewart (eds.), *The Emergence of Evangelicalism: Exploring Historical Continuities* (Nottingham: Apollos, 2008).

on by the name 'Evangelical.'[102] What happened in the mid-eighteenth century is that this part of the Church, depressed by the Laudian victories of the previous century and the moral and spiritual apathy of the time, found renewed vigour. The revivals saw a revivification of the Reformed tradition on which the Anglican Church had originally been founded and which remained a respectable if minority theology within the post-Restoration church.[103] As this tradition was re-energised, along with distinctive doctrines such as justification by grace alone through faith alone, the resulting movement also began to display some of the same doctrinal fractures which had characterised the English church more generally. Specifically, the eighteenth century Evangelicals were divided along the old seventeenth century fault lines between Calvinism and Arminianism. While all Evangelicals claimed to hold to the cardinal tenets of salvation *sola fide* and *sola gratia*, which accounts for the success of their gospel preaching, they also indulged in a revitalised debate on basic theological issues concerning predestination and covenant theology.

For various reasons, these Calvinist controversies have been down-played in much historiography of the period. Bebbington was keen, for example, to describe a united movement centred around his four '–isms'; emphasising the very real divisions amongst the eighteenth century Evangelicals would not have helped develop his founding mythology. Again, in his work on the Church of England, William Gibson develops his own thesis that the eighteenth century church was pervaded by a sense of unity and accord, a general consensus and denominational drift towards a latitudinarian avoidance of conflict. He writes that, "The flight from the damage of the ecclesiastical and political divisions of the seventeenth century is a recurring theme in the sermons and treatises of the period, and churchmen repeatedly sought strategies that would avoid divisions and schism."[104] Hence to put the spotlight on disputes like that between Wesley and Whitefield would be, for him, to give disproportionate emphasis to moments of furious but temporary controversy.

---

[102] See also "Evangelicalism," in F. L. Cross and E. A. Livingstone (eds.), *The Oxford Dictionary of the Christian Church* 2nd ed. (Oxford: Oxford University Press, 1974), 486.

[103] See S. Hampton, *Anti-Arminians: The Anglican Reformed Tradition from Charles II to George I* (Oxford: Oxford University Press, 2008), 272.

[104] W. Gibson, *The Church of England 1688-1832: Unity and Accord* (London: Routledge, 2001), 3.

Evangelical histories and hagiographies also pass over these quarrels, often in a quite perfunctory manner. Their concern is often to highlight the successes of eighteenth century Evangelical heroes in contradistinction to their immediate forebears and their Anglican and Dissenting contemporaries, an agenda not well served by focusing on fundamental disagreements between them. J. C. Ryle, for instance, laments Wesley's Arminianism, yet half of his three short pages on the subject are given over to a quotation from Wesley's funeral sermon for Whitefield in which the disputed points between them are naturally suppressed.[105] Balleine, to take another example, psychologises Whitefield's adoption of the Reformed position on election and alludes briefly to Wesley's sermon against predestination before concluding that, "happily before long the storm blew itself out; better feelings began to prevail; and although the two sections never quite came together again, they continued to work side by side in perfect harmony."[106] How there can be "perfect harmony" between two sides which never come together must remain a mystery. Mark Noll similarly suggests that the Evangelical Calvinists simply reasoned from their experience of grace to their doctrines of predestination. In his brief treatment of the controversies he emphasises the commonalities between both sides and the "significant degree of confluence" between John Wesley and the Calvinist Jonathan Edwards, portraying such disagreements as merely occasional "flash-points."[107]

Evidently contemporary polemical concerns affect each author's selection of emphasis, and perhaps it seems somehow disloyal to the pan-Evangelical cause to highlight Evangelical dissensions. In this chapter, we will first touch briefly on the state of the Church prior to the revival before examining in more depth the first so-called Calvinist controversy between the main Evangelical leaders of the eighteenth century, John Wesley and George Whitefield. This is necessary as a prelude to understanding the single subject of the rest of this study, their contemporary Mr. Toplady, for whom these issues were determinative, decisive, and of constant concern. It is also necessary to be candid and frank about the divisions within the Evangelical Anglican constituency in those days if we are not to

---

[105] J. C. Ryle, *Christian Leaders of the Eighteenth Century* (Edinburgh: Banner of Truth, 1978 [1885]), 85-88.

[106] G. R. Balleine, *A History of the Evangelical Party in the Church of England* (London: Longmans, Green and Co, 1911), 31.

[107] M. A. Noll, *The Rise of Evangelicalism: The Age of Edwards, Whitefield and the Wesleys* (Leicester: Apollos, 2004), 114, 255-260.

lose heart or perspective over similarly deep divisions today.

3.1. *The State of the Church of England before the Revival*

William Hague describes the early eighteenth century church provocatively in his recent biography of William Wilberforce. He speaks of the diluted nature of the Christianity preached in British pulpits, and the "hypocritical and lacklustre way in which it was practised." He describes an ecclesiastical establishment "mired in a period of place-seeking, money-grabbing and moral irrelevance."[108] When William Blackstone, a renowned lawyer at this time, had heard every preacher of note in London he concluded that none of their sermons contained more Christianity than the writings of the pagan philosopher Cicero.[109] After listening to sermons in York, Henry Venn similarly concluded that "excepting a single phrase or two, they might be preached in a synagogue or mosque without offence."[110] One historian of this period candidly asserts that the established religion was regarded by most politicians, and many churchmen too, as merely a valuable form of police control over the lower classes. He goes on to conclude that, "It must be admitted that the church of England during the eighteenth century is not an inspiring spectacle. Latitudinarian to a degree which makes it difficult to find any theological justification for its existence, at its highest it was an efficient instrument of statecraft, at its lowest it was a nest of pluralists and mundane divines."[111]

Pluralism, the practice of a clergyman holding more than one benefice at a time, was rife. One observer lamented that ministry was so under-resourced that poor ministers, unable to secure financially viable benefices, were obliged to take on the cure of souls in several parishes at once simply to survive. This left them, as one observer wrote, "so straiten'd in time by hurrying about from one to another, that they have scarce leisure to read deliberately the prayers at the proper hours of doing it, much less to preach or catechise, or as much as sometimes for to read an homily. Such is the faint shadow that remains among us of the public

---

108 W. Hague, *William Wilberforce: The Life of the Great Anti-Slave Trade Campaigner* (London: Harper Perennial, 2008), 9.

109 An oft-noted observation. See Balleine, *A History of the Evangelical Party*, 11.

110 H. Venn, *The Life and a Selection from the Letters of the late Rev. Henry Venn MA* (London: Hatchard, 1839), 76.

111 B. Williams, *The Whig Supremacy 1714-1760* 2nd ed., revised by C. H. Stuart (Oxford: Clarendon Press, 1960), 76, 87-88.

service of religion."[112] No wonder then that ministers with responsibility for multiple parishes used every short-cut available to them; one entrepreneurial Reverend started a business reprinting the sermons of eminent preachers for the sake of hard-pressed clergy, even printing them in the form of manuscripts (rather than in a book) to save the preacher the trouble of writing out the words in their own handwriting to preserve the illusion.[113]

Those clergy who could acquire lucrative livings often left them in the care of a poorly paid curate while they themselves lived elsewhere off the rump of the proceeds. Such were often portrayed as hard-drinking, nepotistic, and greedy socialites. Above all, writes Hague, "it was the ruthless competition for the most lucrative parishes and dioceses that made the eighteenth century Church a place of touting and toadying ambition, and caused considerable anger amongst a population whose tithe payments funded the generous livings and evident abuses."[114]

There were also, undoubtedly, decent, faithful men labouring in the Lord's vineyard at this time. Indeed, the Anglican church was generally regarded as the bulwark of Protestantism in Europe, and "many European Protestants viewed the Church of England as the principal reformed Church, from which leadership on the issue of unity was expected."[115] This leadership role was not, however, enthusiastically grasped; in 1704 Archbishop Tenison failed to respond, for example, to requests for official ecclesiastical dialogue from German Calvinist leaders. At the same time, at home and abroad, for both humanitarian and religious purposes, dissenters and Churchmen cooperated on the basis of their common Protestant heritage in forming religious societies, such as the Society for Promoting of Christian Knowledge (1698), and the Society for the Propagation of the Gospel (1701).[116] There were external signs of

[112] E. Saunders, *A View of the State of Religion in the Diocese of St. David's About the beginning of the Eighteenth Century. With some account of the causes of its decay* (London, 1721) as extracted in W. Gibson, *Religion and Society in England and Wales 1689-1800* (London: Leicester University Press, 1998), 66.

[113] Hague, *William Wilberforce*, 10. See A. M. Toplady, *The Complete Works of Augustus Toplady* (Harrisonburg, Virginia: Sprinkle Publications, 1987), 869 for an amusing incident where Toplady was offered such ready-made sermons, and J. C. Ryle, *Christian Leaders of the Eighteenth Century* (Edinburgh: Banner of Truth), 365.

[114] Hague, *William Wilberforce*, 10-11.

[115] Gibson, *The Church of England 1688-1832*, 184-185.

[116] Gibson, *The Church of England 1688-1832*, 192.

religious zeal and faithful pastoral care in various parishes.[117]

That being said, such was clearly not the characteristic norm. Toplady once remarked that in the 1720s "a converted minister in the establishment was as great a wonder as a comet."[118] One congregation in Suffolk lamented in 1733 that, "The faithful labourers in Christ's vineyard are so few, and the deceitful and sophisticated corrupters of the word and doctrine so many, that it appears exceedingly difficult for a church really adhering to good old Protestant doctrines to be again settled with a suitable and agreeable Pastor."[119] The problem was not simply the rise of Unitarianism, which had infected many Anglican and Dissenting pulpits. There was a spiritual lethargy in the country at large, which provoked J. C. Ryle in the next century to exclaim, "How such a state of things can have arisen in a land of free Bibles and professing Protestantism is almost past comprehension."[120]

So the earnestness and sincerity and passion of the men who formed the "Holy Club" in Oxford in 1729 was to be their greatest asset. If England was sound asleep, these were the men to wake her up. George Whitefield was initially the most prominent of the new generation of preachers. Everywhere he went he seemed to attract large and emotional crowds with his dramatic style and plain-speaking evangelism. There were many conversions, and considerable controversy. Critics attacked his "enthusiasm," his self-promotion, his critical and sometimes harsh tone towards others in the church, and his itinerant preaching. Yet his methods and manner were copied by others and his message of justification by faith alone quickly spread. After the strange warming of his heart in May 1738, John Wesley also joined the number of those passionately preaching the necessity of the new birth and salvation by grace. This new emphasis was strange to many, and Whitefield and Wesley put some people's noses out of joint by their rather forthright denunciation of existing churches and their apparently lifeless ministries.

Such an approach inevitably led to them not being invited to speak again in many pulpits. Nonetheless, their zeal was strong and so they took

---

[117] See the helpful survey in A. Harding, *Selina Countess of Huntingdon* (Peterborough: Epworth, 2007), 7-9.

[118] See G. M. Ella, *Augustus Montague Toplady: A Debtor to Mercy Alone* (Eggleston, Durham: Go Publications, 2000), 400.

[119] See D. Rosman, *The Evolution of the English Churches 1500-2000* (Cambridge: Cambridge University Press, 2003), 129.

[120] J. C. Ryle, *Christian Leaders of the Eighteenth Century*, 14.

to the streets and the fields, and began open-air preaching. In London one open-air congregation was estimated at 50,000 people. Even in the winter months of 1739 they could pull crowds of 10,000 in Bristol.[121] The numbers may have been a little exaggerated (though not by too much it seems), but clearly there was some kind of revival of interest in the gospel, on both sides of the Atlantic. The Evangelical preachers, or Methodists as they were sometimes known, and those who followed in their wake like William Wilberforce, made a huge impact on British and American society and churches. Some attribute the growth of the Trade Union movement, and the Reform Bill of 1832, to the influence of the revival. Indeed, it has been a common belief since the nineteenth Century that this Evangelical 'awakening' also contributed to the saving of England from the Revolution that had engulfed France.[122]

3.2. *Revival Rivalries*

I mentioned above that Wesley and Whitefield were early on barred from certain pulpits. One of those seems to have been St. Helen's, Bishopsgate, where (if I may speak personally for a moment) I myself worked for five years. More than once I have been told the story of how graceless and dead St. Helen's must have been in those former days, since when John Wesley came to preach one Tuesday lunchtime in May 1738 he wrote in his diary, "My heart was now so enlarged, to declare the love of God, to all that were oppressed by the devil, that I did not wonder in the least, when I was afterwards told, 'Sir you must preach here no more.'"[123] Obviously, it is suggested (as Wesley no doubt intended it to be), the Evangelical doctrine of salvation by God's grace was despised and misunderstood in eighteenth century Bishopsgate.

Yet I was intrigued by this since Wesley had preached at St. Helen's in March that same year (on Luke 9:23) without any adverse

---

[121] A. Dallimore, *George Whitefield: The Life and Times of the Great Evangelist of the 18th Century Revival* Volume 1 (Edinburgh: Banner of Truth, 1970), 289, 263.

[122] See e.g. I. H. Murray, *Wesley and Men Who Followed* (Edinburgh: Banner of Truth, 2003), 102 and D. M. Lloyd-Jones, *The Puritans: Their Origins and Successors* (Edinburgh: Banner of Truth, 1987), 108.

[123] Journal entry for Tuesday 9th May 1738 in T. Jackson (ed.), *The Works of John Wesley* (Grand Rapids: Baker, 2007), 1:93. The Sunday before he had been told something similar by those at nearby St. Lawrence's and St. Katherine Cree, having been "enabled to speak strong words at both."

reaction being reported.[124] Moreover, George Whitefield's journal records that he preached at St. Helen's one Sunday afternoon in August 1736 and had been received far more favourably: "they soon grew serious and exceedingly attentive," he says, "and, after I came down, showed me great tokens of respect, blessed me as I passed along, and made great inquiry who I was."[125]

I was less surprised at the strong reactions against Mr. Wesley, however, when I read the printed version of his sermon on Romans 8:32, the text he preached on at St. Helen's in May 1738. From start to finish it is a sustained, emotive, combative, highly prejudiced and somewhat patronizing rant against Reformed doctrine. He continually rams home his point that believing in predestination is bad for a person's spiritual health and that it destroys all zeal for good works, especially the good work of evangelism. Predestination, he says, is "a doctrine full of blasphemy," and he complains bitterly against "the horrible blasphemies contained in this horrible doctrine." As for particular redemption (or limited atonement), that idea is, "[f]latly contrary to ... the whole tenor of the New Testament." Several proof texts follow in quick succession, without being explained: surely it was simply obvious to all that these texts proved his point, and no sane person could believe in such a doctrine. To those who might disagree with his anti-Calvinist convictions Wesley declared, "You represent God as worse than the devil; more false, more cruel, more unjust... no scripture can prove predestination... I abhor the doctrine of predestination."[126] He then went on to portray those who believe in Reformed doctrine as worse than the baby-sacrificing worshippers of the false god Moloch.

These outbursts are not confined to occasional asides in an otherwise edifying sermon; indeed, they sum up the tenor of the entire discourse. He certainly did not take his own advice, to preach against Calvinism, "though not in a controversial way ... in love and gentleness; not in bitterness ... Rather, mildly expose these things."[127] Reformed

---

[124] *The Works of John Wesley*, 1:85. Wesley's sermon on this text can be found in *The Works of John Wesley*, 6:103-114. It is a milder, more scholarly performance than the Romans 8:32 sermon, with only a brief glance at "Predestinarians" (106).

[125] G. Whitefield, *George Whitefield's Journals: A new edition containing fuller material than any hitherto published* (Edinburgh: Banner of Truth, 1960), 77.

[126] *The Works of John Wesley*, 7:380-383.

[127] "Minutes of Several Conversations between the Rev. Mr. Wesley and others, from the year 1744, to 1789," in *The Works of John Wesley*, 8:336.

sympathies would, therefore, be clearly on the side of the discerning pastor or churchwarden who sought to protect St. Helen's, which had a history of solidly Reformed ministry, from hearing such divisive and melodramatic things again.[128] The printed edition of the sermon states that it was "preached at Bristol in the year 1740," and it has been asserted that Wesley had no interest in opposing Calvinism before that date,[129] but there is little reason to doubt it was substantially the same as the London sermon given on the identical text in mid-1738. Before the Bristol sermon was first preached, for example, Wesley was already known as an anti-Predestinarian, and had been warned by several people (including Whitefield) not to stir up trouble by preaching against it.[130] It is highly likely that this was because he had already done so elsewhere. Itinerant evangelists are not known for re-writing entire sermons for different congregations, and we know that the revivalists re-used their texts many times; Wesley preached his sermon on Matthew 16:26 on literally hundreds of occasions, for example.[131] It seems more than possible, then, that a draft of Wesley's famous sermon against predestination had an outing in Bishopsgate in 1738 before it gained its notoriety in Bristol a year later and was subsequently published.

In April-May 1739 Wesley's journals allude to his teaching again on Romans 8:32 and on passages well known as key texts in the Arminian case against Calvinism. He preached repeatedly on 1 Timothy 2:3-6, "God desires all people to be saved and to come to the knowledge of the truth... Christ Jesus gave himself as a ransom for all," as well as John 1:29, "the

---

[128] See Gatiss, *The Tragedy of 1662*, 30, 39, 43-48 on Arthur Barham, the Presbyterian Vicar of St. Helen's, who had been ejected in 1662. The sermons of one of his late seventeenth century successors, Dr. Thomas Horton, also demonstrate that predestination, penal substitution, particular atonement, the imputation of the active obedience of Christ, irresistible grace, the importance of promiscuous gospel preaching to all, and the necessity of the new birth were all previously proclaimed in the same City pulpit from which Wesley asserted his Arminianism in 1738. See e.g. T. Horton, *Forty-six Sermons upon the Whole Eighth Chapter of the Epistle of the Apostle Paul to the Romans* (London, 1674), 9-14, 50, 501-503. That Erasmus Middleton, a graduate of Kingswood School, one of the six students ejected from Oxford because of his Calvinistic Methodism in 1769, and Toplady's successor as editor of the Calvinist *Gospel Magazine*, was also a Lecturer at St. Helen's, reveals something of where the church was theologically in the eighteenth century.

[129] R. Burrows, *John Wesley in the Reformation Tradition: The Protestant and Puritan Nature of Methodism Rediscovered* (Stoke-on-Trent: Tentmaker, 2009), 39.

[130] See A. Dallimore, *George Whitefield: The Life and Times of the Great Evangelist of the 18th Century Revival* Volume 2 (Edinburgh: Banner of Truth, 1980), 20 and 1:307.

[131] See Burrows, *John Wesley in the Reformation Tradition*, 202.

lamb of God who takes away the sin of the world," and 1 John 2:1-2, "Jesus Christ the righteous is the propitiation for our sins, and not for ours only but also for the sins of the whole world."[132] These are the very texts he more than once cites in his written works as proofs against reprobation and particular atonement.[133] Clearly, this was not just an emphasis in Wesley's preaching prior to his Aldersgate experience (the St. Helen's sermon was on 9th May 1738 and his heart was not "strangely warmed" until 24th May). Rather, like his mother, he had strong Arminian sentiments from very early on, which he tenaciously held onto all his life.[134] As Iain Murray concludes, "The truth is that Wesley's opposition to Calvinism stiffened rather than weakened."[135]

He never mentions Arminianism or Calvinism in his journals at this stage, but it seems clear what he was attempting to do. He protests when some in Bristol accuse him of being "a Papist, if not a Jesuit,"[136] but his defensive protestations about his doctrine of justification by faith alone perhaps hide the true cause of the accusation: alongside justification *sola fide* he had quite deliberately been preaching the distinctives of Arminianism, and for well over a century such doctrine had been intimately linked in the public mind with a Romewards tendency, as we have already observed. His published journals obviously do not expound this somewhat covert strategy, but he was forming a bridgehead into the nascent Evangelical movement and the banners around which he was able to rally his own following were anti-Calvinism and his doctrine of Christian perfectionism. He may not reveal the details of his plan, but he was less than subtle in his determined prosecution of this agenda. While Whitefield went on a preaching tour to America, Wesley very effectively swooped in to take over the movement, putting himself at its head, as Dallimore demonstrates in sordid detail.[137]

In 1741, to counter the influence of Whitefield after his return, Wesley published eleven separate tracts and books directly related to these

---

[132] *The Works of John Wesley* 1:188-193.

[133] See *The Works of John Wesley*, 7:381 and 10:214-215.

[134] On the Arminianism of Susannah Wesley (whose father was a nonconformist minister in the parish of St. Helen's, Bishopsgate), see M. Wellings, "Susannah Wesley, 1669-1742," in A. Atherstone (ed.), *The Heart of Faith: Following Christ in the Church of England* (Cambridge: Lutterworth, 2008), 64-65 and Murray, *Wesley and Men who Followed*, 57-58.

[135] Murray, *Wesley and Men who Followed*, 68.

[136] See *The Works of John Wesley*, 1:218-219.

[137] See Dallimore, *George Whitefield* 1:306-319 and 2:18-41.

divisive topics, including a third edition of the *Free Grace* sermon on Romans 8:32, several treatises on predestination from an Arminian perspective, a sermon on Christian Perfection, and hymnbooks extolling blatant anti-Calvinism and scurrilous pieces called "The Cry of a Reprobate" and "The Horrible Decree" designed to mock and caricature Reformed views.[138] Given this clear agenda zealously pursued, it is rather strange (though not uncharacteristic) for Wesley to blame Whitefield and others who held to particular redemption for the breach in Methodism at this point.[139]

Julia Wedgwood's nineteenth century biography of Wesley makes the rather insightful comment that Wesley's *Free Grace* sermon has "in it something of that provoking glibness with which young or half-cultivated people settle in a few sentences questions that have exercised the deepest minds ever since the dawn of speculation... Indeed, it is evident on reading this sermon that, of all the deep works which had been written on the subject, Wesley had never read one; he had taken it for granted that the opinion he set himself to confute could be held by none but fools, and his confutation was condemned to that futility by which all such arrogance is punished."[140] Wesley's line, however, was that God told him to oppose predestination. He had cast lots and received very clear guidance to "preach and print" against predestination. This was not an unusual method of finding divine guidance for a man who often simply opened the Bible at random looking for a lead.[141] But Wesley tried to use this supposed divine mandate to pressurize booksellers into stocking it, claiming not only sanction from on high to print the sermon but that God's blessing was evident when he preached it.[142]

3.3. *Whitefield's Reformed Response*

These things hurt Whitefield privately and publicly. He would often have to distance himself publicly from Wesley in future. Yet 30 years later, Charles Wesley (his opponent's brother) was able to pay Whitefield this touching tribute:

---

[138] See Dallimore, *George Whitefield* 2:68 for details of the publishing schedule.

[139] *The Works of John Wesley*, 8:349.

[140] J. Wedgwood, *John Wesley and the Evangelical Reaction of the Eighteenth Century* (London: Macmillan, 1870), 226-227.

[141] See Dallimore, *George Whitefield* 1:273. In *The Works of John Wesley*, 1:160 he finds relief from perplexity by randomly opening the Bible to the notorious Prayer of Jabez.

[142] See Wesley's letter to James Hutton in Dallimore, *George Whitefield* 1:314.

> Though long by following multitudes admired,
> No party for himself he e'er desired;
> His one desire, to make the Saviour known,
> To magnify the name of Christ alone:
> If others strove who should the greatest be,
> No lover of pre-eminence was he,
> Nor envied those his Lord vouchsafed to bless,
> But joy'd in theirs, as in his own success,
> His friends in honour to himself preferr'd,
> And least of all in his own eyes appear'd.[143]

Whitefield pleaded with Wesley not to publish the offending sermon. When Wesley ignored him, Whitefield felt constrained, very reluctantly, to offer a reply to the sermon, in a public letter to Wesley.[144] It was clear, courteous, and effective. Moreover, like his earlier private letters to Wesley on the subject, it was very restrained and mildly put in comparison with Wesley's bitter invective, especially when that is read in the context of Wesley's shenanigans in attempting to hijack and take over Whitefield's movement while he was abroad. Whitefield clearly *had* read some deep works on the subject, and he refers Wesley to them several times. He also pointed out to his friend that,

> Had any one a mind to prove the doctrine of *election*, as well as of *final perseverance*, he could hardly wish for a text more fit for his purpose, that that which you have chosen to disprove it. One that does not know you would suspect you yourself was [*sic*] sensible of this: for after the first paragraph, I scarce know whether you have mentioned it so much as once, through your whole sermon.[145]

Whitefield rebukes Wesley's lack of attention to the text he claimed to be expounding. Romans 8:32 was a classic text used to underpin (rather than undermine) Calvinist doctrine, and not just on election and perseverance but also on limited atonement. This is how it had been used by, for

---

[143] From *The Journal of Charles Wesley* Volume 2, 428 as quoted in Dallimore, *George Whitefield*, 2.519. Charles disagrees with his mother here, who wrote that Whitefield was jealous of her sons. See C. Wallace (ed.), *Susanna Wesley: The Complete Writings* (New York: Oxford University Press, 1997), 466.

[144] The text is reprinted in Dallimore, *George Whitefield* 2:551-569 and *George Whitefield's Journals*, 563-588. See also several earlier private letters in Dallimore, *George Whitefield*, 1:571-581.

[145] Dallimore, *George Whitefield* 2:555; emphasis original.

instance, Thomas Horton of St. Helen's, Bishopsgate in his sermon on it published in 1674.[146] As Whitefield said, universal atonement must surely imply universal salvation.[147] Far from being the doctrine of narrow-minded, stay-at-home preachers, Calvinist doctrine was held by godly men of "catholic spirit" who longed to see people converted. Unconditional election was a daily comfort to believers, a strong motivation to holiness of life, and a spur to evangelism. This is warm piety allied to solid theology, all served up in a firm but friendly tone.

Wesley, who obviously identified Whitefield with the wider Reformed tradition, wrote that no Baptist or Presbyterian writer he had read knew anything of the liberties of Christ.[148] Whitefield counters this by arguing that Wesley's sermon associated him with a different tradition: "universal redemption [atonement] is a notion sadly adapted to keep the soul in its lethargic sleepy condition, and therefore so many natural men admire and applaud it... Infidels of all kinds are on your side of the question. Deists, Arians, Socinians, arraign God's sovereignty, and stand up for universal redemption."[149] He then cites Article 17 to show that "our godly reformers did not think election destroyed holiness" and questions Wesley's loyalty to the Reformed Church of England saying, "I cannot but blame you for censuring the clergy of our church for not keeping to their articles, when you yourself by your principles, positively deny the 9th, 10th, and 17th."[150]

It is worth reminding ourselves at this point what these Articles teach on the disputed points. Article 9, for example, was contrary to Wesley's doctrine of original sin, affirming that,

> Original sin standeth not in the following of Adam, (as the Pelagians do vainly talk,) but it is the fault and corruption of the nature of every man, that naturally is ingendered of the offspring of Adam, whereby man is very far gone from original righteousness, and is of his own nature inclined to evil, so that the flesh lusteth always contrary to the spirit; and therefore in every person born into this world, it deserveth God's wrath and

---

[146] See Horton, *Forty-six Sermons*, 527-528. See S. Jeffery, M. Ovey, A. Sach, *Pierced for our Transgressions: Rediscovering the Glory of Penal Substitution* (Nottingham: IVP, 2007), 272 for a modern deployment of this text in a similar context.
[147] Dallimore, *George Whitefield* 2:567-568.
[148] Dallimore, *George Whitefield* 2:564.
[149] Dallimore, *George Whitefield* 2:560, 565.
[150] Dallimore, *George Whitefield* 2:559, 569.

> damnation. And this infection of nature doth remain, yea in them that are regenerated... the Apostle doth confess that concupiscence and lust hath of itself the nature of sin.

Article 10 takes a very clear line on free will, affirming that humans have no such thing after the Fall and are totally unable to even prepare themselves for faith or good works in their own strength:

> The condition of man after the fall of Adam is such that he cannot turn and prepare himself by his own natural strength and good works to faith and calling upon God; wherefore we have no power to do good works pleasant and acceptable to God, without the grace of God by Christ preventing [i.e. preceding] us, that we may have a good will, and working with us, when we have that good will.

Article 17 is the longest of all the Thirty-nine Articles, and the one most clearly against Wesley's position. It shows that the Reformers considered predestination a vital subject which needed to be correctly defined and taught for the church's doctrinal and pastoral health. It begins, alluding to Romans 9-11 and Ephesians 1,

> Predestination to life is the everlasting purpose of God, whereby (before the foundations of the world were laid) he hath constantly decreed by his counsel secret to us, to deliver from curse and damnation those whom he hath chosen in Christ out of mankind, and to bring them by Christ to everlasting salvation, as vessels made to honour.

It continues by outlining the *ordo salutis*, or order of salvation, experienced by the elect, in the manner of Romans 8:28-30, emphasising the free, gracious, merciful nature of God the Trinity's preservation of the saints from election all the way to glory:

> Wherefore they which be endued with so excellent a benefit of God be called according to God's purpose by his Spirit working in due season; they through grace obey the calling; they be justified freely; they be made sons of God by adoption; they be made like the image of his only begotten Son Jesus Christ; they walk religiously in good works and at length by God's mercy, they attain to everlasting felicity.

Article 17 then continues by countering those who thought it best not to discuss such high and lofty matters. Much was lost if predestination was not preached, discussed, and meditated upon:

> As the godly consideration of predestination, and our election in Christ, is full of sweet, pleasant and unspeakable comfort to godly persons, and such as feel in themselves the working of the Spirit of Christ, mortifying the works of the flesh and their earthly members, and drawing up their mind to high and heavenly things, as well because it doth greatly establish and confirm their faith of eternal salvation to be enjoyed through Christ, as because it doth fervently kindle their love towards God...

Such is the positive and warm official opinion of the Church of England about this neglected and despised doctrine. There is then the note of how this doctrine, especially its negative implications, can be abused. The darker side of predestination is not denied here, of course (Wesley was right in his sermon, that election and rejection must go together). Yet there is a way of misusing what the Bible says on this point:

> ... so for curious and carnal persons, lacking the Spirit of Christ, to have continually before their eyes the sentence of God's predestination, is a most dangerous downfall, whereby the Devil doth thrust them either into desperation, or into wretchlessness of most unclean living, no less perilous than desperation.

The antidote was simply never to preach reprobation (the negative "sentence of God's predestination") as an excuse for immorality. God's decrees are, in any case, "secret to us," and while believers can contemplate their election in Christ, sinful unbelievers cannot know for sure this side of judgment day what God has decreed for them. They may yet be converted: Christ Jesus came into the world precisely to save sinners (1 Timothy 1:15). The minister's task, therefore, is to declare the revealed promises of scripture to all sinners, as applicable to anyone who comes to Christ by faith:

> Furthermore, we must receive God's promises in such wise as they be generally set forth to us in Holy Scripture; and in our doings, that will of God is to be followed which we have expressly declared to us in the Word of God.

Whitefield's response, affirming these specific Articles 9, 10, and 17 against Wesley, places him firmly in the mainstream Reformed tradition of the Church of England. He was a firmly convinced Anglican, upholding the biblical basis and usefulness of the Articles, Liturgy, and

Homilies.[151] That these "essential articles of the Church of England, which undoubtedly are Calvinistical," had been neglected for so long he considered "one of the greatest judgements that has befallen our nation."[152]

Whitefield very effectively draws on Reformed Anglicans of previous generations in his reply to Wesley, without even mentioning John Calvin (or John Owen). He claimed to hold the doctrines of grace because he found them in the Bible and that Jesus taught them: "Alas, I have never read anything that Calvin wrote; my doctrines I had from Christ and His apostles; I was taught them of God."[153] Yet he was also influenced by reading and meeting other Calvinists. He was a particular fan of seventeenth century Cambridge theologian, John Edwards (not to be confused with Whitefield's American contemporary Jonathan Edwards).[154] Edwards (1637-1716) was a noted Anti-Arminian Churchman,[155] who at that start of his classic Reformed Evangelical Anglican book *Veritas Redux: Evangelical Truths Restored* wrote,

> I have taken care to satisfy every unprejudiced person, that that which we now call Calvinism, is to be found in the writings of the ancient fathers of the Church, and is the very doctrine which the first reformers of our own Church professed, and maintained, and which is contained in our Articles, Homilies and liturgy, and which our Archbishops and Bishops, and the whole body of our English clergy have generally asserted and vindicated.[156]

Such was Whitefield's own belief, and more than one of Edwards' books was on his list of the most important works of divinity, alongside other classic Reformed works by Matthew Henry, Thomas Boston, John Pearson, John Owen, and John Bunyan.[157] *Veritas Redux* is in fact cited

---

[151] See e.g. *George Whitefield's Journals*, 249-50, 256, 286. On the Homilies see his Preface to a projected new edition of the Homilies in *The Works of the Reverend George Whitefield: Volume IV* (London, 1771), 441-444.

[152] *The Works of the Reverend George Whitefield: Volume IV*, 115.

[153] Dallimore, *George Whitefield*, 1:574 from a letter to Wesley dated Aug 25th 1740.

[154] See Dallimore, *George Whitefield* 1:405 for Edwards' influence and 404-409 on Whitefield's Calvinism generally.

[155] See Hampton, *Anti-Arminians*, 21-22,

[156] J. Edwards, *Veritas Redux: Evangelical Truths Restored* (London, 1707), xix.

[157] See *The Works of the Reverend George Whitefield: Volume III* (London, 1771), 497-498 and Volume IV, 306-307.

twice in Whitefield's open letter to Wesley,[158] and Wesley came to dislike Edwards intensely.[159] Whitefield was also in harmony with the Reformed tradition in general, holding as he did to the inseparability of justification and sanctification,[160] the imputation of the active obedience of Christ,[161] the perseverance of the saints,[162] and identifying Arminianism as "anti-Christian" and tending to Popery.[163] No wonder when he returned from Georgia and met Wesley in April 1741 he told him plainly face-to-face that they "preached two different gospels."[164] He was equally candid later in his ministry with Count Zinzendorff, often associated with the Methodists, when he felt important lines had been crossed, being astonished at the Moravian's use of images of Christ, incense, and other superstitious and idolatrous practices.[165]

Whitefield's Reformed credentials are also revealed by the use he makes of the Reformed doctrine of the covenant. He is happy to speak, for example, in classic Reformed fashion, about the covenant of works,[166] and the covenant of grace.[167] These were key anchor points in the puritan and Reformed overview of the Bible. Less noticed perhaps is the use he makes of the covenant of redemption, or *pactum salutis* — the teaching that the covenant of grace by which humans are saved in history is based on an eternal covenant between the members of the Trinity, or as seventeenth century theologian John Owen put it, "the ground of... Christ's being punished for us... is that compact, covenant, convention, or agreement, that was between the Father and the Son, for the accomplishment of the

---

[158] Dallimore, *George Whitefield* 2:553, 567. See also 1:575 where he recommends Edwards to Wesley in another letter dated Sept 25th 1740.

[159] See *The Works of John Wesley,* 1:294.

[160] E.g. L. Gatiss (ed.), *The Sermons of George Whitefield: Part 1* (Watford: Church Society, 2010), 276. *Select Sermons of George Whitefield* (Edinburgh: Banner of Truth, 1958), 132.

[161] E.g. *The Sermons of George Whitefield: Part 1,* 266, 273-274 and L. Gatiss (ed.), *The Sermons of George Whitefield: Part 2* (Watford: Church Society, 2010), 221. *Select Sermons,* 107, 120, 129-130.

[162] E.g. *The Sermons of George Whitefield: Part 2,* 220, 439, 458. *Select Sermons,* 88, 106, 196.

[163] E.g. *The Sermons of George Whitefield: Part 1,* 263, 267, 274. *Select Sermons,* 116, 121, 129.

[164] *The Works of John Wesley,* 1:305.

[165] See *The Works of the Reverend. George Whitefield: Volume IV,* 253-261 (in a letter from April 1753).

[166] E.g. *The Sermons of George Whitefield: Part 1,* 263, 266 and *Part 2,* 215, 433. *Select Sermons,* 81, 100, 116, 119.

[167] E.g. *The Sermons of George Whitefield: Part 2,* 221. *Select Sermons,* 107.

work of redemption."[168]

There were many precursors to this covenant of redemption idea in early Reformed theology. Arminius himself had made use of the idea of a covenant between the Father and the Son,[169] but the more developed Reformed doctrine of the *pactum salutis* was formulated from the mid-seventeenth century onwards with explicit anti-Arminian motives. It specifically addressed the special love of God for the elect, offering an eternal foundation for this in an intra-trinitarian covenant. Some have attacked it as being "mythology" and inimical to the Trinity,[170] or as having no real biblical basis.[171] Richard Muller has convincingly shown, however, that it arose not only out of polemical and theological reflection but concerted examination of a whole series of biblical texts.[172] As Carl Trueman rightly says, "the point is established in Reformed Orthodoxy by careful linguistic reflection upon the biblical text, not simply some kind of apriorism or dogmatic straitjacketing."[173]

Emphasis on the *pactum* was really about getting the biblical story right rather than merely a concern of abstract systematizing. It is about seeing where the narrative of God's grace and love for the world begins,

---

[168] J. Owen, *Vindiciae Evangelicae* in W. H. Goold (ed.), *The Works of John Owen* (Edinburgh: Hunter and Johnson, 1850-1853), 12:496-497. See also the Savoy Declaration VIII.1.

[169] See R. A. Muller, "Toward the *Pactum Salutis:* Locating the Origins of a Concept," *Mid-America Journal of Theology* 18 (2007), 12-13 n14. See also H. Witsius, *The Economy of the Covenants Between God and Man Comprehending a Complete Body of Divinity* trans. W. Crookshank Volume 1 (London, 1822 [1693]), 176 on Arminius.

[170] K. Barth, *Church Dogmatics* ed. G. W. Bromiley and T. F. Torrance (Edinburgh: T&T Clark, 1956-1973), IV/1, 65 and II/2, 78. See the Reformed critique of Barth's view in G. J. Williams, "Karl Barth and the Doctrine of the Atonement," in D. Gibson and D. Strange (eds.), *Engaging Barth: Contemporary Evangelical Critiques* (Nottingham: IVP, 2008), 271.

[171] E.g. R. T. Beckwith, "The Unity and Diversity of God's Covenants," *Tyndale Bulletin* 38 (1987), 99 n23. For an outline of other modern critiques, including those of T. F. Torrance, J. Murray, and O. Palmer Robertson, see J. Mark Beach, "The Doctrine of the *Pactum Salutis* in the Covenant Theology of Herman Witsius," *Mid-America Journal of Theology* 13 (2002), 105-115.

[172] Muller, "Toward the *Pactum Salutis,*" 19, 21, 25-46, 64. The texts he mentions include Psalm 2:7, Psalm 40, 45, 110; Isaiah 11, 42:1-6, 49:1-2, 53:10-12, 55:3-4, 54:10; Luke 22:29; Galatians 3:16-17; Ephesians 1:4-7; John 6:37-45; 1 Peter 1:20, and a whole host of passages in Hebrews, especially chapters 7-9.

[173] C. R. Trueman, *John Owen: Reformed Catholic, Renaissance Man* (Aldershot: Ashgate, 2007), 83. Owen also considered the accusation that it led to tritheism. See the helpful exposition of Owen's doctrine in R. W. Daniels, *The Christology of John Owen* (Grand Rapids: Reformation Heritage Books, 2004), 153-167.

so that we can properly appreciate the climaxes and consummation of his plan in the death, resurrection, ascension, and second coming of the Lord Jesus Christ. It is part of the romance of the gospel. Indeed, Charles Spurgeon called this doctrine of the intra-trinitarian covenant, "a noble and glorious thought, the very poetry of that old Calvinistic doctrine which we teach."[174] Jim Packer is bold enough to say that, "The full reality of God and God's work are not adequately grasped till the Covenant of Redemption — the specific covenantal agreement between Father and Son on which the Covenant of Grace rests — occupies its proper place in our minds."[175]

In the nineteenth century, George Smeaton commented that, "This doctrine has fallen out of the prominence it at one time occupied in theology."[176] Yet that was certainly not yet the case for Whitefield in the eighteenth century. Whitefield is not only aware of this doctrine but deploys it on several occasions in precisely the anti-Arminian contexts for which it seems to have been developed. So, for example, he writes to Wesley, "But, blessed be God, our Lord knew for whom he died. There was an eternal compact between the Father and the Son. A certain number was then given him, as the purchase and reward of his obedience and death. For these he prayed, John xvii, and not for the world. For these, and these only, he is now interceding, and with their salvation he will be fully satisfied."[177] He also reveals this exegetically-based, Reformed framework to his thinking in several of his sermons. For example, while preaching on 1 Corinthians 1:30 (a text Wesley had used in Bristol many times during his fiercely Arminian takeover),[178] he proclaims,

> There was an eternal contract between the Father and the Son: 'I have made a covenant with my chosen, and I have sworn unto David my servant'; now David was a type of Christ, with whom the

[174] See C.H. Spurgeon, "The Blood of the Everlasting Covenant," (Sermon 277) at http://www.spurgeon.org/ (accessed 18-07-09).

[175] J. I. Packer, "On Covenant Theology," in *Celebrating the Saving Work of God: Collected Shorter Writings of J. I. Packer Volume 1* (Carlisle: Paternoster, 1998), 17. See also pages 15-16 where he shows how this doctrine very effectively counters false teaching such as the "distressing nonsense" of "the tritheistic fantasy of a loving Son placating an unloving Father and commandeering an apathetic Holy Spirit in order to save us."

[176] G. Smeaton, *The Doctrine of the Atonement as Taught by Christ Himself* (Edinburgh: T&T Clark, 1868), 375.

[177] Dallimore, *George Whitefield* 2:568.

[178] See *The Works of John Wesley*, 1:186, 192, 203 "my favourite subject," 211-212. Wesley's sermon does not seem to have been preserved.

> Father made a covenant, that if he would obey and suffer, and make himself a sacrifice for sin, he should 'see his seed, he should prolong his days, and the pleasure of the Lord should prosper in his hands.' This compact our Lord refers to, in that glorious prayer recorded in the 17th chapter of John; and therefore he prays for, or rather demands with a full assurance, all that were given to him by the Father.[179]

This was no small detail for Whitefield. "Would to God this point of doctrine was considered more," he says, "and people were more studious of the covenant of redemption between the Father and the Son!" Then, in an aside clearly aimed against Wesley and other Arminian Evangelicals, he says if people were more attentive to the eternal covenant between the members of the Trinity, "We should not then have so much disputing against the doctrine of election, or hear it condemned (even by good men) as a doctrine of devils. For my own part, I cannot see how true humbleness of mind can be attained without a knowledge of it; and though I will not say, that every one who denies election is a bad man, yet I will say... it is a very bad sign... for, if we deny election, we must, partly at least, glory in ourselves."[180]

This emphasis in Whitefield's preaching was not just evident in the heat of the Calvinist controversies; it is part of how he conceives of and preaches the gospel message. Speaking on Genesis 3:15 about the difference between the covenants of works and redemption he says,

> This is by no means an unnecessary distinction; it is a matter of great importance: for want of knowing this people have been so long mislead. They have been taught that they must do so and so, as though they were under a covenant of works, and then for doing this, they should be saved. Whereas, on the contrary, people should be taught, That the Lord Jesus was the second Adam, with whom the Father entered into covenant for fallen man; that they

---

179 *The Sermons of George Whitefield: Part 2*, 212. *Select Sermons*, 96-97. Note the allusions here to Psalm 89, Isaiah 53, and John 17. A modern exposition of the biblical basis for the *pactum salutis* can be found in A. J. Köstenberger and S. R. Swain, *Father, Son and Spirit: The Trinity and John's Gospel* (Nottingham: IVP, 2008), 169ff.

180 *The Sermons of George Whitefield: Part 2*, 212-213. *Select Sermons*, 97-98. For the "doctrine of devils" accusation see Dallimore, *George Whitefield*, 1:577.

can do nothing of or for themselves.[181]

In his final sermon in England on August 30th 1769, speaking of Christ's love for his people, Whitefield declares, "We are his eternal election: 'the sheep which thou hast given me,' says Christ. They were given by God the Father to Christ Jesus, in the covenant made between the Father and the Son from all eternity." Characteristically, however, he immediately went on to say, "They that are not led to see this, I wish them better heads; though, I believe, numbers that are against it have got better hearts: the Lord help us to bear with one another where there is an honest heart."[182] He referred of course to John Wesley, who disliked the idea of the *pactum salutis.*[183] Clearly the breach with Wesley, though he attempted time and again to heal it, was a source of ongoing tension for Whitefield until the very end.

3.4. Conclusion

It is absolutely essential for a proper understanding of the Evangelical Revival to grasp the depth and significance of the cleavage between Wesley and Whitefield on the Arminian question. For both men these were issues that affected them personally and (so to speak) professionally throughout their relationship and the debates they occasioned were not merely "flash-points" that can be easily ignored, but of profound importance to their ministries. Thirty years after Wesley used his intemperate sermon to successfully divide and conquer the movement Whitefield began, both men had matured theologically in very different directions.

J. I. Packer once wrote of Wesley that he was "a confused Calvinist" because he shared with Whitefield a belief in promiscuous gospel preaching and the necessity of holiness; and his brother Charles' hymn *And Can It Be?* can be sung quite vigorously by Calvinists.[184] Two

---

[181] *The Sermons of George Whitefield: Part 1*, 57. *Select Sermons*, 154-155. He here recommends *A View of the Covenant of Grace* by Scottish theologian Thomas Boston (1676-1732), a key Calvinist player in the Marrow Controversy within Scottish Presbyterianism also praised in *Eighteen Sermons Preached by the late Rev. George Whitefield A.M.* (London, 1771), 322.

[182] *The Sermons of George Whitefield: Part 2*, 452. *Select Sermons*, 190.

[183] See e.g. *The Works of John Wesley*, 10:238-239, 324-325, 422-423.

[184] "Predestination in Christian History," in *Collected Shorter Writings of J. I. Packer: Honouring the People of God* (Carlisle: Paternoster, 1999), 215-216; originally published in 1983.

years later, however, he wrote a scholarly exposé of Wesley's Evangelical Arminianism that was more careful in describing the tensions in Wesley's theology.[185] Wesley was at heart an Arminian but, happily, an inconsistent one. Tensions and incoherencies are inevitable when a man who "abhors" predestination also wants (rightly) to assert the Reformation doctrine of justification by grace alone through faith alone. This certainly distinguishes such 'Evangelical Arminianism' from the more thoroughgoing 'rationalistic' Arminianism of Laud and others in the previous century, and enabled a degree of cooperation in mission, on occasion, between the Wesleys and Whitefield. Yet Wesley's High Church background, and family history (he was brought up to despise Calvinism and his puritan heritage), not to mention his links with the Moravians and trips to Lutheran Germany, meant he was always predisposed to take a different line.

George Whitefield on the other hand, though he was rather prone to some dramatic excesses in his early years, was a much less confused and confusing figure. His early biblical convictions on the doctrines of grace were strengthened by reading Reformed Evangelical Anglicans and the puritans, as well as by visiting Reformed Baptists and Presbyterians in America and Scotland. Those links to other parts of the English-speaking world, where Calvinism remained more respectable than in England itself, became increasingly important for him. Yet because there was a continuous indigenous Reformed tradition within the established church, however low its fortunes had sunk, it was possible for the Evangelical revival to take on a strongly Reformed character in many parts of England. Indeed during the revival, as Hampton says, "it was the Reformed who were the majority amongst the conforming evangelicals."[186] Of these Whitefield was always the most famous and revered being not only a powerful preacher but also, as Toplady said, "a most excellent systematic divine."[187] Though Wesley always had the advantage in terms of organizational ability and empire building, Whitefield's Reformed theology gave his message and ministry a depth and stability that Wesley somehow lacked.

---

[185] See "Arminianisms," in *Honouring the People of God*, 302; originally published in 1985.

[186] Hampton, *Anti-Arminians*, 273.

[187] A. M. Toplady, *The Complete Works of Augustus Toplady* (Harrisburg, Virginia: Sprinkle Publications, 1987), 494. Contra H. S. Stout, *The Divine Dramatist: George Whitefield and the Rise of Modern Evangelicalism* (Grand Rapids: Eerdmans, 1991), 39 who says "he showed no interest in theology"!

Whitefield was diligent in seeking reconciliation with Wesley. This did not prove to be easy, though some years later he was able to cooperate with Wesley in some ways, uniting around the great principles of the gospel which they held in common, even when their underlying theological understanding and rationale differed widely.[188] While they retained some "catholic spirit" there was hope for an Evangelical alliance across the very serious Calvinist-Arminian divide, if the fiery rhetoric could be dialed down. Charles Wesley summed up this mood:

> Ah! wherefore did we ever seem to part,
> Or clash in sentiment, while one in heart?
> What dire device did the old serpent find,
> To put asunder those whom God had joined?
> From folly and self-love opinion rose,
> To sever friends who never yet were foes;
> To baffle and divert our noblest aim.[189]

John Wesley, on the other hand, was in deadly earnest as he wrote about Calvinism, "All the devices of Satan, for these fifty years, have done far less toward stopping this work of God than that single doctrine." He advised his preachers to seize upon the newly converted in order to guard them from "the predestinarian poison," and to "make it a matter of constant and earnest prayer, that God would stop the plague."[190] So the atmosphere was soon to change within Evangelical circles after Whitefield's death in 1770 seemed to leave Wesley without serious rival.

---

[188] See Dallimore, *George Whitefield*, 2.139-147, 335-353.

[189] See J. L. Schwenk, *Catholic Spirit: Wesley, Whitefield, and the Quest for Evangelical Unity in Eighteenth-Century British Methodism* (Plymouth: Scarecrow Press, 2008), 125.

[190] "Minutes of Several Conversations," in *The Works of John Wesley*, 8:336-337.

4. Augustus Montague Toplady: A Reformed Evangelical Anglican

I never felt so intense a desire to be useful to the souls of my people; my heart was expanded, and burnt with zeal, for the glory of God, and for the spiritual welfare of my flock. I wished to spend and be spent in the ministry of the word, and had some gracious assurances from on high that God would make use of me to diffuse his gospel, and call in some of his chosen that are yet unconverted.

- Toplady's *Journal*, 28th August 1768

We now turn to scrutinize the work of one specific Evangelical in the Anglican Reformed tradition: Augustus Montague Toplady (1740-1778). His short life was lived right in the centre of the Evangelical awakening: as he was born, Jonathan Edwards was experiencing 'the distinguishing marks of a work of the Spirit of God' in New England, Whitefield was building the Bethesda Orphanage in Savannah, Georgia and Wesley was preaching "Free Grace" in Bristol. Toplady outlived Edwards by twenty years and Whitefield by eight, but Wesley continued to make an impact until his death in 1791. Toplady is best known today as the writer of hymns such as 'Rock of Ages' and a 'A Debtor to Mercy Alone,' which is perhaps not inappropriate since he lived in a famously musical age, his life overlapping with Vivaldi, Bach, Handel, and Mozart. In his own day, however, he was equally famous (or perhaps notorious) as a Reformed theologian and controversialist. His theological concerns fit comfortably into the polemical framework established in the previous century but he engaged John Wesley with a particular passion in an effort to rebut his distinctive teachings.

In this chapter we will examine Toplady's theological identity, first as an Evangelical believer and preacher, then as a Reformed theologian, and finally as an Anglican churchman. This will enable us in the next chapter better to unpack his Reformed Evangelical Anglican polemic against Wesley and therefore to observe something of the heartbeat of conforming Calvinism during the eighteenth century revival. At the heart of everything for Toplady was "the true profession of the gospel."

4.1. *Toplady as an Evangelical*

Toplady's 'coming to faith' at the age of 15 certainly appears to have all the hallmarks of a classic Evangelical conversion narrative. Enjoying his first summer vacation as a student of Trinity College, Dublin in August 1756 the scholarly Augustus (former student of the prestigious Westminster school in London, and already the published author of some religious poems) found himself in a barn with some Irish peasants listening to James Morris, one of Wesley's itinerants. A dozen years later he recalls the scene in his journal:

> That sweet text, Ephes ii 13, was particularly delightful and refreshing to my soul; and the more so, as it reminded me of the days and months that are past... It was from this passage that Mr. Morris preached on that memorable evening of my effectual call by the grace of God. Under the ministry of that dear messenger, and by that sermon, I was, I trust, brought nigh by the blood of Christ... Strange that I, who had so long sat under the means of grace in England, should be brought nigh in an obscure part of Ireland, amidst a handful of God's people, met together in a barn, and under the ministry of one, who could hardly spell his name! Surely it was the Lord's doing and it was marvellous! ... The regenerating Spirit breathes not only on whom, but likewise when, where, and as he listeth.[191]

He had not been without pious thoughts and prayers before 1756 and had even written hymns,[192] but he wrote to James Morris in 1768 to encourage him, saying, "God made you the means of my conversion twelve years ago... How has my heart burnt within me, and how have my tears flowed, like water from the smitten rock, when I heard you preach the unsearchable riches of his grace, blood and righteousness! The word came with power, and with the Holy Ghost sent down from heaven."[193] *Amazing Grace* was not published until after Toplady died, but he would surely have echoed its sentiments and sung it with all his might: "how precious did that grace appear, the hour I first believed."

---

[191] A. M. Toplady, *The Complete Works of Augustus Toplady* (Harrisburg, Virginia: Sprinkle Publications, 1987), 2.

[192] See his juvenile diaries for 1752-1754 in G. M. Ella, *Augustus Montague Toplady: A Debtor to Mercy Alone* (Eggleston, Durham: Go Publications, 2000), 416-425.

[193] *Complete Works*, 831.

If Toplady's conversion was 'Evangelical,' what of his connections? During his student days in Ireland, as well as being a communicant of the established church he was in touch with Baptists, Moravians, Independents, and several Methodists. He may even have met Wesley himself at this time, and he certainly corresponded with him more than once.[194] From his memoirs, it seems he grew to be a particular admirer and friend of the Baptist John Gill, but no-one held higher place in his esteem than George Whitefield. Toplady called him, "the apostle of the English empire... a most excellent systematic divine... the prince of preachers."[195] His letters reveal that Toplady was also on friendly terms with other Evangelical leaders of the revival including, of course, the Countess of Huntingdon,[196] (whom he called "the most precious saint of God I ever knew"),[197] the scholar-preacher William Romaine,[198] and John Berridge of Everton in Bedfordshire.[199] He was certainly a part of the circle of Evangelical leadership during the mid eighteenth century.

Toplady's Evangelical experience can be observed in his hymns, letters, and journal. These reveal a believer with something of a Spirit-orientated piety: he often spoke of the Spirit's work in his life, guiding and sanctifying, and wrote a hymn "to the blessed Spirit."[200] He speaks of "the faithfulness of the Holy Ghost, who, when once given, is a fountain of living water, springing up in the believer's heart to life eternal," and of being led by "the still, small whisper of his good Spirit," to whom he attributed all his love, gratitude, and sanctification.[201] Whitefield once said that "the grand controversy God has with England is for the slight put on the Holy Ghost. As soon as a person begins to talk of the work of the Holy Ghost, they cry, you are a Methodist: as soon as you speak about the divine influences of the Holy Ghost, O! say they, you are an enthusiast."[202]

---

[194] See G. Lawton, *Within the Rock of Ages: The Life and Work of Augustus Montague Toplady* (Cambridge: James Clarke and Co, 1983), 28-31.

[195] *Complete Works*, 494. See also in Toplady's sermon on Isaiah 55:12 in Ella, *Augustus Montague Toplady*, 400.

[196] *Complete Works*, 862-3, 872-3.

[197] *Complete Works*, 876.

[198] His letters to Romaine are in *Complete Works*, 848, 854, 858.

[199] See *Complete Works*, 874.

[200] *Complete Works*, 910 "Holy Ghost, dispel our sadness." See also pages 896 "Earnest of future bliss," and 908 "Come Holy Ghost, our souls inspire."

[201] *Complete Works*, 8. The repeated mentions of the Spirit on this one page seem indicative of his general mindset.

[202] *Eighteen Sermons Preached by the late Rev. George Whitefield A.M.* (London, 1771), 381-382.

In this context we can easily see how Toplady would be regarded as amongst the Evangelicals.[203]

If the Spirit taught Toplady anything it was to revel in Christ. He rejoiced that, "one moment's communion with Christ, one moment's sense of union with him, one moment's view of interest in him, is ineffable, inestimable!"[204] He was a man utterly seized by a godly activist ambition, writing that, "There are, that I know of, but two things worth living for: 1. To further the cause of God, and thereby glorify him before the world; 2. To do good to the souls and bodies of men."[205] Although he was aware that others might think his experience smacked of 'enthusiasm,'[206] he seems conscious of having an immanent sense of intimate and continual relationship with God, and his diary entries are full of pious prayer and thought, sometimes recording particular encouragements from his morning Bible reading,[207] and suffused with the intense relational language of Song of Songs.[208] Yet he was not without blacker moments too, being equally honest about these "doubts and fears and unbelief... I seemed to have quite lost my hold on the rock of ages... almost in a state of despair."[209] As Arthur Pollard so memorably puts it, Toplady's faith, "was faith in the furnace, religion at perpetual white heat."[210]

The Revd. A. M. Toplady considered himself an Evangelical minister,[211] and sometimes used the adjective "unevangelical" as an insult.[212] As an Evangelical he was particularly keen on the ministry of the

---

[203] Though he did not own the name 'Methodist,' since he considered Methodism a "virulent sect" led by John Wesley. See *Complete Works*, 840.

[204] *Complete Works*, 11. See also his quotation of "Mr. Lee's choice sermon" concerning gradual acquaintance with all three members of the Trinity on page 10.

[205] *Complete Works*, 9.

[206] See *Complete Works*, 6, 19.

[207] E.g. *Complete Works*, 16.

[208] E.g. *Complete Works*, 16, 20.

[209] *Complete Works*, 20.

[210] A. Pollard, 'Toplady, Augustus Montague (1740–1778),' *Oxford Dictionary of National Biography* (Oxford: Oxford University Press, 2004).

[211] By implication, see *Complete Works*, 7.

[212] *Complete Works*, 12.

word, which he considered "an authority which cannot err."[213] Arguably following Article 21, which specifically contrasts erring human authority with scripture ("God's word written," Article 20), other Anglican Evangelicals also held this view of the Bible's entire trustworthiness.[214] When he, "burnt with zeal, for the glory of God, and for the spiritual welfare of my flock," he declared, "I wished to spend and be spent in the ministry of the word, and had some gracious assurances from on high that God would make use of me to diffuse his gospel, and call in some of his chosen that are yet unconverted."[215] He was very much against "too curious speculation," telling one friend that "God's word is the believer's chart; God's Spirit is the believer's pilot."[216] He generally preached up to 45-50 minutes, it seems, often to large afternoon congregations in his church at Broad Hembury. He approved of the advice he heard from an old dissenting minister that preaching ought to dwell chiefly on Christ, not controversies, and urging preachers to, "endeavour to preach more to the hearts of your people than to their heads" and "seek rather to profit than to be admired."[217] This did not stop him from being a powerful preacher, as one account of his oratory makes clear:

> As a public speaker he stood eminently distinguished. Never did a man ascend the pulpit with a more serious air, conscious of the momentous work that he was engaged in. His discourses were

---

[213] *Complete Works*, 646. See also 311, "God's unerring oracles," and 389, "the Bible is the unerring word of God," and 664, "the unerring word," and 735 for, "The Holy Spirit, making the apostle's pen the channel of unerring inspiration," and 745 for the epistles and Gospels "written under the unerring influence of the same Holy Spirit," and 769, "oracles of unerring truth." For the related concept of infallibility see 342 where he also calls the Bible "that unerring standard." Interestingly, some editions of the *Book of Common Prayer*, including those published in Dublin in 1750, 1753, and 1757 (while Toplady was a student at Trinity College), spoke of God's "unerring word" in their version of the Psalms, e.g. at Psalm 119:81 and 119:114.

[214] See e.g. L. Gatiss (ed.), *The Sermons of George Whitefield: Part 1* (Watford: Church Society, 2010), 73 and *Select Sermons of George Whitefield* (Edinburgh: Banner of Truth, 1958), 174 for "the unerring rule of God's most holy word." James Hervey in his 'Contemplation on the Starry Heavens,' in *Meditations and Contemplations: Volume 2* (1748), 227 speaks of the Word of God as 'this unerring directory,' and of its 'infallible guidance.' John Newton in *Letters, Sermons, and a Review of Ecclesiastical History* (1780), 246 (Letter 20) and 324 (Letter 32) writes of 'the unerring word of God.' See also the Church of England's Homily 22 which describes the Bible as "his infallible word."

[215] *Complete Works*, 25.

[216] *Complete Works*, 848. See also 363, "the ministry of the word being the principal reaping-hook which God's Spirit makes use of" for sanctification and conversion.

[217] *Complete Works*, 25.

> extemporary, delivered in strains of true unadulterated oratory. He had a great variety of talents, such as are seldom seen united in one person: his voice was melodious and affecting; his manner of delivery and action were engaging, elegant, and easy, so as to captivate and fix the attention of every hearer. His explanations were distinct and clear; his arguments strong and forcible; and his exhortations warm and animating; his feelings were so intensely poignant, as to occasion, in some of his addresses, a flow of tears.. Notwithstanding he was possessed of whatever study and application could impart, or learning, judgment, and genius could combine, we find him estimating all human attainments as of little consequence in divine things, without the effectual agency of the Holy Spirit.[218]

Toplady also records some of the details of his personal ministry with individuals, such as William Taylor the local farmer. The young vicar regularly visited Taylor, who did not have long to live. On one occasion he reports the West Country farmer's confidence in Christ, and it pleased the minister greatly when the old man reported, "my pains are nothing to my hopes."[219] Toplady was sure a work of grace had begun in him, and also in two ladies who seem to have been strong supporters of his ministry, "good old Mrs. Hutchings," and an illiterate spinner called Joan Venn.[220] Even with his privileged education and "capacious soaring mind,"[221] he seems to have been able to reach people in every station of life with the gospel.

Finally, it would be remiss not to glance at the cross-centred nature of so many of Toplady's poems and hymns as evidence of his Evangelical convictions. Quite apart from his justly famous line, "nothing in my hand I bring, simply to thy cross I cling," his crucicentrism can be seen on almost every page of his poetical works. Consider for example his sense of wonder at the cross:

> And did the Saviour thus exchange
> His throne of glory for a cross?
> Left he for this th'ethereal court,

---

[218] A. C. H. Seymour, *The Life and Times of Selina, Countess of Huntingdon: Volume 2* (London, 1840), 63-64.

[219] See *Complete Works*, 22-23.

[220] See *Complete Works*, 22, 26-28.

[221] Seymour, *The Life and Times of Selina*, 64.

To die a painful death for us?
For us he bled at ev'ry vein,
And, slain by man, for man was slain.[222]

We also hear his clear Evangelical doctrine of penal substitutionary atonement:

For me vouchsaf'd the unspotted Lamb
His Father's wrath to bear:
I see his feet, and read my name
Engraven deeply there.[223]

also in a hymn called *the Propitiation*:

Thy anger, for what I have done,
The gospel forbids me to fear:
My sins thou hast charg'd on thy Son:
My justice to him I refer.

Be mindful of Jesus and me!
My pardon he suffer'd to buy;
And what he procur'd on the tree,
For me he demands in the sky.[224]

and another based on Hebrews 10:19:

Our scarlet crimes are made as wool,
And we brought near to God:
Thanks to that wrath-appeasing death;
That heav'n-procuring blood.[225]

He often uses the biblical idea of the cross as example:

Resolv'd to tread the sacred way
That Jesus water'd with his blood,
I bend my fix'd and cheerful course
Through that rough path my master trod.[226]

---

[222] *Complete Works*, 905 "Look back, my soul," verse 4.
[223] *Complete Works*, 905 "Redeem'd offender, hail the day," verse 3.
[224] *Complete Works*, 909-910.
[225] *Complete Works*, 910 "O precious blood, O glorious death," verse 4.
[226] *Complete Works*, 906, "Can ought below engross my thought?" verse 3.

and also as a victory:

The pow'r of hell, the strength of sin,
My Jesus shall subdue:
His healing blood shall wash me clean,
And make my spirit new.[227]

The cross also invites sinners to come home to God:

Draw near with Faith, ye doubting Souls,
'Tis the Redeemer calls you Home:
His Blood invites all Sinners here,
And cries, incessant, 'there is Room.'[228]

this message being one that should be heard throughout the world:

In thy Gospel-Chariot, Lord,
Drive through Earth's utmost Bound;
Spread the Odour of thy Word
Through all the Nations round.[229]

So to conclude, his conversion, his connections, his 'charismatic' experience, his calls to the converted and unconverted and his cross-centred hymnody all testify that Toplady was an Evangelical, however defined. As Paul Helm says, he "presses most of the right Bebbingtonian buttons" (conversionism, activism, biblicism, crucicentrism).[230] Yet, as we shall see, he clicks on Calvinism much more firmly and in his self-understanding is decidedly Reformed.

4.2. *Toplady as Reformed*

At the age of 18, Toplady underwent an experience he later ranked as second only to his conversion. Though he was awakened to Evangelical faith at the age of 15, Toplady declares, "I was not led into a full and clear view of all the doctrines of grace, till the year 1758, when, through the

[227] *Complete Works*, 913 verse 1 of a hymn called *Divine Aid*.

[228] A. M. Toplady, *Hymns and Sacred Poems on a Variety of Divine Subjects* (London: Daniel Sedgwick, 1860), 103 in a hymn called *For the Sacrament* (verse 1) which echoes some of the words of administration in the 1662 Communion liturgy and also invites participants there to "renew your covenant with God" (verse 5).

[229] *Complete Works*, 891 "Bring the kingdom, Lord, make haste," verse 2.

[230] P. Helm, "Calvin, A.M. Toplady and the Bebbington Thesis," in M. A. G. Haykin and K. J. Stewart (eds.), *The Emergence of Evangelicalism: Exploring Historical Continuities* (Nottingham: Apollos, 2008), 219.

great goodness of God, my arminian prejudices received an effectual shock."[231] This profound jolt was administered through his reading of some sermons on John 17 by puritan preacher Thomas Manton,[232] and a work of systematic theology by Zanchius (of which more later). He said afterwards that he would remember these two dates, the year of his conversion and the year he realised Arminianism was unbiblical, "with gratitude and joy, in the heaven of heavens, to all eternity."[233]

Toplady was exceptionally well read in a wide variety of subjects and engaged closely with authors beyond his own tradition, especially those like Peter Heylyn who had written voluminously against the doctrinal and historical positions Toplady adopted.[234] Nevertheless, he expressed special admiration for particular authors who he linked with the anti-Arminian / anti-Pelagian cause. Amongst those was "the great Calvin," whose *Institutes* he ranked as "one of the most admirable compositions which any age has seen."[235] Yet he was no slavish imitator or acolyte of the Genevan Reformer, being immersed in a far broader Reformed (as opposed to merely Calvinian) tradition. One of his favourite books, cited around a hundred times in *The Historic Proof of the Doctrinal Calvinism of the Church of England* is "Mr. Fox's inestimable Martyrology,"[236] a solidly Reformed and Protestant work. As well as Foxe, he greatly admired Scottish Reformer John Knox, Protestant apologist John Jewel, and Synod of Dort delegate George Carleton.[237] He esteemed puritans such as John Bunyan very highly,[238] and though he was not always entirely positive about the puritans as a whole (the terms puritan, noncomformist, and Calvinist not being for him synonymous),[239] he considered the great ejection of 1662 to be, "a blow to vital religion, to the

---

[231] *Complete Works*, 34-35.

[232] The sermons can be read in volumes 10 and 11 of T. Manton, *The Complete Works of Thomas Manton* (Vestavia Hills, Alabama: Solid Ground, 2008).

[233] *Complete Works*, 35 and the similar recounting on 850.

[234] See *Complete Works*, 58, 64, 103, 160 for just a few of the many citations of Heylyn "that virulent polemicist," (142) in *The Historic Proof.* Toplady outlines his view of Heylyn himself in a huge footnote, 624-625 note u.

[235] *Complete Works*, 70 note g and 81 note d.

[236] *Complete Works*, 122.

[237] See his biographies of these men in *Complete Works*, 451-468. For his very positive assessment of the Synod of Dort see 238, 633 and A. Milton (ed.), *The British Delegation and the Synod of Dort (1618-1619)* Church of England Record Society Volume 13 (Woodbridge, Suffolk: The Boydell Press, 2005), xx.

[238] *Complete Works*, 12.

[239] *Complete Works*, 272-274, 637.

protestant interest in general, and to the Church of England herself... the fatal extinguishment of so many burning and shining lights" which "gave the true Church of England so severe a bleeding that she has never entirely recovered herself from that time to this."[240]

He spoke highly of Post-Restoration Reformed Anglicans such as Bishops William Beveridge and John Pearson, and Dr. John Edwards of Cambridge (as well as his more famous non-Anglican near namesake Jonathan Edwards of New England).[241] He was also an enthusiastic reader of continental Protestant theology particularly the Italian Reformer Jerome Zanchius and the Dutch Reformed scholastic Hermann Witsius, of whom his fellow-Evangelical James Hervey was also a passionate admirer.[242] According to Toplady, the Genevan theologian Francis Turretin was "one of the greatest divines that ever lived."[243] Amongst his near contemporaries he was a devotee of the Scottish Presbyterian Ebenezer Erskine, the Particular Baptist John Gill, and of course George Whitefield.[244] Perhaps surprisingly though, "the prince of divines" as far as Toplady was concerned was Archbishop Thomas Bradwardine (1290-1349),[245] and he devotes several pages in *The Historic Proof* to the mediaeval prelate.[246] Indeed, he writes concerning pre-Reformation England that,

> From among the ancient worthies, natives of our own land, and remarkable for having been led into an acquaintance with the distinguishing doctrines of the gospel; Bede, Grosthead, Wickliffe, Bradwardin, and Lord Cobham, may be selected, as none of the least conspicuous. If our island be disgraced with having given birth to Pelagius, she is also honoured with having been the mother of such sons as have cut up Pelagianism both root and branch.[247]

---

240 *Complete Works*, 10, 479.

241 See e.g. *Complete Works*, 258-260, 748 note d, 750 note e, 864.

242 See I. Rivers, 'Hervey, James (1714–1758),' *Oxford Dictionary of National Biography* (Oxford: Oxford University Press, 2004).

243 See *Complete Works*, 669-675 for his view of Zanchy; 81 note d, 470-479, 854 on Witsius; 64 on Turretin.

244 *Complete Works*, e.g. 12, 25 (Erskine); 3, 4, 7, 14 (Gill); and 494 (Whitefield).

245 *Complete Works*, 494, 840.

246 *Complete Works*, 104-113. See also 517.

247 *Complete Works*, 99. In the previous century, John Owen had also singled out Bradwardine for special mention in the centuries long struggle against Pelagianism, in his Preface to T. Gale, *The True Idea of Jansenisme* (London, 1669).

Thus Toplady linked his doctrinal understanding with the cream of the Reformed community in Europe and Britain, and sought to show that this was part of an anti-Pelagian heritage stretching back well before the Reformation. Though he was literally near-sighted,[248] Toplady was anything but theologically myopic. Indeed, he was so bold as to assert that before the arch-heretic Pelagius (c.354-420) Christians were "unanimous believers of the doctrines now termed Calvinistic."[249] This broad historical view was developed in sharp distinction to Heylyn's Laudian polemic which not only attempted to portray Arminianism as the key principle of the original Reformation but also accused Calvinists of only being able to trace their pre-Reformation ancestry through a series of heterodox mediaeval sects.[250] For Toplady, anti-Pelagianism was the very essence of Calvinism, and so he was delighted to find it in mainstream figures such as Bede and Bradwardine as well as in Wycliffe, the more radical dissident.[251]

Toplady's major doctrinal loyalties and concerns can be seen throughout his body of work. Naturally as a Reformed Protestant he was a faithful defender of the catholic (universal) creeds and their basic Trinitarianism. Beyond that, his anti-Pelagianism played itself out in his doctrines of free will, original sin, and predestination. He considered gratuitous unconditional election to be, along with the Trinity, one of the master pillars of the church.[252] God has chosen an innumerable, "exceeding great" multitude for glory,[253] while others are chosen for death he says (citing 2 Corinthians 4:3, 1 Peter 2:8, 2 Peter 2.12, Jude 4, and Revelation 17:8). As an infralapsarian, however, he can assert that the condemnation of the non-elect is just and fair because they are considered in God's decree not merely as 'neutral' people but as fallen, rebellious

---

[248] *Complete Works,* 843.

[249] *Complete Works,* 80, 612. See also W. H. Goold (ed.), *The Works of John Owen* (Edinburgh: Johnstone and Hunter, 1850-55), 7:75.

[250] See for example his *Historia Quinqu-Articularis: or, a Declaration of the Judgement of the Western Churches; and more particularly the Church of England in the Five Controverted Points; Reproached in these last times by the name of Arminianism, Part II* (London, 1660), 8-9 where he typically attacks Wycliffe, but also Toplady's favourite, John Foxe. According to A. Milton, *Laudian and Royalist Polemic in Seventeenth-Century England: The Career and Writings of Peter Heylyn* (Manchester: Manchester University Press, 2007), 15, 20-22, 68, 207, 228 undermining Calvinists on 'church succession' was a key part of Heylyn's polemical strategy.

[251] In *Complete Works,* 133 he directly equates Calvinists with anti-Pelagians.

[252] *Complete Works,* 303.

[253] *Complete Works,* 726, 736.

sinners, who are condemned on the basis of their sin.[254]

He often criticises the alternative Reformed position (supralapsarianism) as being too "highly Calvinistic," since for him it appears to make God the author of sin,[255] though he concedes that some of the best and greatest men have held to this view, which is tolerable in the Church of England system.[256] Yet he is clearly opposed to the Roman Catholic doctrine of predestination on the basis of foreseen works.[257] This was shared by Arminians such as Wesley, who said clearly in his *Predestination Calmly Considered* that, "I believe election means... a divine appointment of some men to eternal happiness. But I believe this election to be conditional... unconditional election I cannot believe."[258] In other words, God foresaw who would respond to the gospel call and chose them, on that basis.[259]

In his treatise 'calmly' considering predestination, Wesley asserts that no-one is damned for original sin.[260] Toplady teaches just the opposite, refuting this Arminian doctrine using the standard covenantal terms of Reformed theology.[261] Man is born in sin, and bound in sin. On the question of the human will Toplady was in fundamental agreement with Luther's teaching (though not his style) in his book against Erasmus, that the will is not free or sovereign.[262] The dispute was not about the existence of human will but its power, Toplady said, writing, "The grand hinge, then, on which the debate turns, is, whether free-will be, or be not, a faculty of such sovereignty and power, as either to ratify, or to baffle, the saving grace of God, according to its own independent pleasure and self-determination? I should imagine, that every man of sense, piety, and reflection, must, at once, determine this question in the negative."[263]

Toplady was amazed that anyone could thus affirm their own will's independent ability and power to convert themselves or to win over

---

[254] *Complete Works*, 746.
[255] See this criticism in e.g. *Complete Works*, 204, 612-613, 627.
[256] *Complete Works*, 125 note u.
[257] *Complete Works*, 175.
[258] T. Jackson (ed.), *The Works of John Wesley* (Grand Rapids: Baker, 2007), 10:210.
[259] *The Works of John Wesley*, 10:218. See also the "free grace" sermon, *The Works of John Wesley*, 7:380, 385.
[260] *The Works of John Wesley*, 10:223.
[261] See "A Short Essay on Original Sin," in *Complete Works*, 409-416.
[262] *Complete Works*, 155, 613-614, 679. See also 69 on Luther's violent and coarse language.
[263] *Complete Works*, 112.

temptation apart from God. He continues, "When free-willers kneel down to petition God for any spiritual blessing, what is such conduct but a virtual renunciation of their own distinguishing tenet? [There is no] more glaring example of human inconsistency than a free-willer on his knees."[264] This was confirmed in his own experience of conversion, and he used that common Christian testimony when trying to persuade others on this point.[265] There is, though, no violent compulsion in God's converting us, stressed Toplady; he preferred to speak of invincible rather than irresistible grace, since "An elect sinner is not made good against his will, but is by grace made willing to be good."[266]

Thus far Toplady appears as a mainstream Reformed theologian. In addition to Reformed views of election, original sin, and free will he also held to the preservation of the saints,[267] the third use of the Law (as a guide for Christians to live by),[268] and the imputation of the active and passive righteousness of Christ to the believer.[269] He also held to some minority positions within the Reformed consensus. Along with William Twisse, the prolocutor of the Westminster Assembly, and John Gill, Toplady held to the doctrine of justification from eternity, in his early days at least.[270] Along with the sixteenth century Reformer Bishop Hooper, he also taught indiscriminate infant salvation, whereas other Reformed theologians were more cautious about speaking of salvation outside the covenant.[271] He used this doctrine in a variety of polemical and no doubt also pastoral ways. For example, he implies the superiority of his Reformed view of infant salvation when he asks "what becomes of departed infants upon the Arminian plan of conditional salvation, and

---

264 *Complete Works*, 112-113.

265 See the story of Toplady's encounter with an older Christian who quizzed him about his conversion in *Complete Works*, 355 (in a sermon entitled "Free-Will and Merit Fairly Examined: or, Men Not Their Own Saviours,") which he also employs in conversation with an Arminian (842-843). For a modern use of the same argument concerning praying for others to be converted see J. I. Packer, *Evangelism and the Sovereignty of God* (Downers Grove, IL: IVP, 1991 [1961]), 15-16.

266 *Complete Works*, 638.

267 E.g. *Complete Works*, 360.

268 *Complete Works*, 309-310, 367.

269 E.g. *Complete Works*, 310.

270 *Complete Works*, 7.

271 See the taxonomy of Anglican and Reformed views in B. B. Warfield, "The Development of the Doctrine of Infant Salvation," in *Studies in Theology, The Works of Benjamin B. Warfield: Volume 9* (Grand Rapids: Baker, reprinted 2003), 427-434.

election on good works foreseen."[272] How can they fulfil any conditions or perform any good works through their free will, as Arminianism seemed to require? If Arminian opponents portray election as a monstrous thing because it would reprobate tiny infants, Toplady replies that he not only believes the rubric in the *Book of Common Prayer* that baptised children who die before committing actual sin are undoubtedly saved but goes further, holding that "all departed infants whatever, whether baptized or unbaptized, are with God in glory."[273] Calvinism is far from the "gloomy" thing it is presented to be by critics such as Dr. Priestley — "Is it gloomy to believe that the far greater part of the human race are made for endless happiness?" he writes to the famous scientist, especially considering that half the population die in infancy and of their salvation there can be no reasonable doubt.[274]

To conclude, then, Toplady considered himself a part of a grand tradition of anti-Pelagianism in line with "all the reformed and evangelical churches abroad."[275] He was happy to confess that some great and good men did not think as he did on these points,[276] and yet to be Reformed and Evangelical was to his mind not only biblically faithful but more fruitful as well. In the early days of his ministry, he wrote to the Countess of Huntingdon, "I dwelt, chiefly, on the general outlines of the gospel," fearful of going any further into difficult theological ground. Yet as he began to preach more about predestination, "or, in other words, of tracing salvation and redemption to their first source," he found a much greater response: "The consequence of my first plan of operations was, that the generality of my hearers were pleased: but very few were converted. The result of my latter deliverance from worldly wisdom and from worldly fear... is, that multitudes have been very angry: but the conversions which God has given me reason to hope he has wrought have been at least three for one before."[277] *Town and Country Magazine*, which gave him the nickname, "The Predestined Parson," reported that Toplady's change of preaching style from 'moralistic' to 'enthusiastic' (as they termed it) led to him being "followed from all parts of the town, and his congregations were so numerous that... there was an overflow almost as soon as the

[272] *Complete Works*, 58.
[273] *Complete Works*, 645-646.
[274] *Complete Works*, 863.
[275] *Complete Works*, 207.
[276] *Complete Works*, 275.
[277] *Complete Works*, 862.

doors were opened."[278]

4.3. *Toplady as an Anglican*

Toplady was not, however, merely an Evangelical Reformed minister. He was also proud to be a clergyman of the established church. For him as a Reformed believer it was a great comfort that the Thirty-nine Articles were clearly Augustinian, "a plain transcript of St. Austin's doctrine, in the controverted points of original sin, predestination, justification by faith alone, efficacy of grace, and good works."[279] In 1770 he declared in a sermon, "I have subscribed to the Articles, Homilies, and Liturgy, five separate times; and that from principle: nor do I believe those forms of sound words because I have subscribed to them: but I therefore subscribed them because I believed them." The Church of England was, he said, "the best and purest visible church in the whole world."[280]

The Predestined Parson made it clear, however, that though he was Calvinist his agreement with Geneva did not extend to issues of church polity; hence the name of his magnum opus is *The Historic Proof of the Doctrinal Calvinism of the Church of England*, the word "doctrinal" being far from superfluous. Government by bishops was not strictly necessary for a true church; that is, as later writers put it, episcopacy is not of the *esse* of the church, only its *bene esse*.[281] Yet, says Toplady, "In nothing did the wisdom of our reformers more strikingly appear, than in connecting the purest doctrines with the best form of ecclesiastical government and discipline."[282] He added that this was, "A species of discretion, in which the foreign leaders of the reformation were not so happy," though he also thought that there was some desire for and even envy of Reformed episcopacy amongst the Reformed on the continent, even from Calvin himself.[283]

Since he was in friendly correspondence with several leading dissenters from the national church, it is important to note how Toplady the Anglican orientated himself with regard to these free churches. His

---

278 "Memoirs of the Predestined Parson," *Town and Country Magazine* (Supplement for 1777), 676.
279 *Complete Works*, 125.
280 *Complete Works*, 311. See also 610, 651.
281 See e.g. T. Bradshaw, *The Olive Branch: An Evangelical Anglican Doctrine of the Church* (Carlisle: Paternoster, 1992), 175.
282 *Complete Works*, 125.
283 *Complete Works*, 125, 207-208.

view of their gospel orthodoxy, and his collaboration with them, prompts William Gibson (outrageously) to label Toplady "heterodox."[284] He outlines his position regarding the dissenting churches in an important letter to "Mr. F" in November 1777. He had been asked about a situation where the gospel is not preached in the local Anglican church but *is* preached in a nonconformist congregation nearby. Toplady replied to his enquirer that faced with this situation, "if he cannot hear the church of England doctrines [i.e. the Reformed faith, "the gospel of grace,"] preached in a parish church (which is terribly the case in some thousands of places), he is bound in conscience to hear those truths where they can be heard: was it in a barn, in a private house, in a field, or on a dunghill." He did think, however, that there was no reason for such a person to absent himself from Communion services in the parish church, especially considering the excellence of the liturgy which the clergy were forced to use with "its admirable and animating form of sound words." He himself had followed this path for several years after his conversion and was convinced "that this was pleasing to God." He concluded with these striking words:

> I am thoroughly persuaded, was the glorious company of apostles to live again on earth at this very time, and to live in England, not one of them, I verily believe, would be a dissenter from our established church: though they would all deeply lament the dreadful state of spiritual, of doctrinal, and of moral declension, to which the greatest part of us are reduced.[285]

The Countess of Huntingdon was keen to secure Toplady's services, and George Whitefield had encouraged him to itinerate. Yet he was content to remain mostly in the small sphere to which God had assigned him, preaching in a few parish churches, saying, "I consider the true ministers of God as providentially divided into two bands: viz., the regulars and the irregulars." Some such as Whitefield were akin to cavalry and others, like him, were more like sentinels or guardsmen watching over a more circumscribed district.[286] He could see the great blessing that the irregular and unusual ministry of men like Whitefield had been, but did not think it was for him, or for everyone; an ordinary Reformed Evangelical parochial ministry within the Church of England structures was just as

---

[284] W. Gibson, *The Church of England 1688-1832: Unity and Accord* (London: Routledge, 2001), 203.

[285] *Complete Works*, 879.

[286] *Complete Works*, 862.

vital and important as the more high-profile 'celebrity' roles.

Toplady had impeccable Anglican credentials and experience as former curate of Blagdon in Somerset and Farleigh Hungerford near to Bath, and as Vicar of Harpford and Venn Ottery, and finally of Broad Hembury, all villages in Devon. Due to ill health he was advised to move to London, and while there he was able to occupy the pulpit of the French Calvinist Chapel in Orange Street for the last three years of his life. He was a prime example, therefore, of a firmly Anglican minister whose Reformed foundations also enabled him to move amongst Reformed nonconformists of various kinds, and be accepted by them, with truly 'ecumenical' ease.

The eighteenth century saw an increase in the activity of a number of sub-Christian groups, such as Arians and Socinians. We have already noted in a previous chapter how some of the Presbyterian and Congregational churches had become fatally infected with these deviant forms of non-Trinitarian belief in the years following the great ejection. In such a context, Toplady was convinced that clerical subscription to the Thirty-nine Articles was of prime importance in guarding the doctrinal boundaries of the established church. He once attended an Arian meeting led by a former Anglican clergyman and reported this to a friend saying, "I never prized our good old liturgy, and the precious doctrines of the reformation, more than on hearing Mr. Lindsey's liturgy and sermon yesterday... it was mere Lindsey throughout: absolute Arianism, Socinianism, and Pelagianism."[287]

In 1771, an infamous meeting at the Feathers Tavern called for the abolition of clerical subscription to the Thirty-nine Articles.[288] Toplady wrote a stinging rebuke to those who wished to continue in the pay and employ of the Church long after they had abandoned her doctrinal commitments: "Let them retract their subscriptions, not by word and in tongue only, but in deed and in truth, by renouncing the preferments, as well as the doctrines, of the church; and all the world will call them honest

---

[287] *Complete Works*, 857.

[288] See Gibson, *The Church of England 1688-1832*, 208. See also 19-20 on anti-subscriptionism. This movement had friends in high places and was supported by various clergy and academics with Socinian leanings including John Jebb, Fellow of Peterhouse, Cambridge. Another Old Petrean, the Duke of Grafton, who was Prime Minister (1768-1770) and Lord Privy Seal (1771-1775), was also a prominent eighteenth century Unitarian.

men."[289] He was no intolerant persecutor, however, declaring, "Keep Antitrinitarians out of the Church by all means: but let them enjoy every advantage of civil society; together with the free exercise of their religion, only *extra ecclesiam*, not within the establishment." The same applied to nonconformist ministers, who were still required to subscribe to most of the Articles in order to enjoy legal toleration. He was also in favour of abolishing the requirement that undergraduates must subscribe: "As if men could not be able lawyers, physicians, or musicians, without being orthodox."[290]

We can observe something of Toplady's attachment to the Church of England in his defence of the doctrine of the *pactum salutis*, the intra-trinitarian pact which stood behind the covenant of grace. As we have already seen, Whitefield and others held this view of covenant theology, which had developed more fully amongst the Reformed during the later seventeenth century. It was a way of connecting classic orthodox Trinitarian theology with the historical accounts and teaching of Christ in the Gospels, often with a conscious effort to blend doctrinal and redemptive-historical perspectives.[291] For Toplady, the agreement and harmony of the godhead in our salvation is a commonplace, and he often speaks in three-fold Trinitarian terms.[292] Yet he also speaks more precisely of "the eternal covenant of grace, which obtained among the persons of the godhead" and of "the everlasting covenant of the uncreated three" which he more often than not links with the related doctrines of election and particular redemption.[293] He often writes of "the covenant of redemption and grace," as if the eternal intra-Trinitarian covenant and the covenant of God with man were very closely related, if not identical, like Scottish theologian Thomas Boston who said, "The covenant of redemption and the covenant of grace, are not two distinct covenants, but

289 *Complete Works*, 302. See also 311 where he accuses such people of "subscribing to articles they do not believe, merely for the sake of temporal profit or aggrandisement."

290 *Complete Works*, 306.

291 See C. R. Trueman, *John Owen: Reformed Catholic, Renaissance Man* (Aldershot: Ashgate, 2007), 87 and J. Mark Beach, "The Doctrine of the *Pactum Salutis* in the Covenant Theology of Herman Witsius," *Mid-America Journal of Theology* 13 (2002), 103.

292 E.g. *Complete Works*, 313, 319, 882.

293 *Complete Works*, 116, 427. See also 415, 882. He is not embarrassed to use the word 'covenant' to describe this inter-trinitarian economy as some have been. See J. Murray, *Collected Writings of John Murray* Volume 2 (Edinburgh: Banner of Truth, 1977), 130-131.

one and the same covenant... under different considerations."[294]

Toplady normally includes the Spirit in this pre-temporal arrangement.[295] Trueman notes a role for the Spirit in John Owen's doctrine of the covenant of redemption,[296] though he does not appear in Owen, or other seventeenth century Reformed theologians such as Cocceius, as an actual contracting party to the eternal covenant.[297] Indeed, Jonathan Edwards specifically ruled this out in his formulation of the *pactum*.[298] Other Evangelical Anglicans, however, such as William Romaine, took Toplady's fully Trinitarian position, speaking of the covenant of the Trinity or of "the Eternal Three" before all worlds.[299] In all probability, Toplady owes this distinctive emphasis on the Spirit in the eternal covenant to his Reformed Baptist friend John Gill, who wrote that the Spirit, "was not a mere by-stander, spectator and witness of this solemn transaction, compact and agreement, between the Father and the Son, but was a party concerned in it."[300] Toplady incorporates this thought into the Trinitarian structure of his hymn *The Method of Salvation*,

---

[294] T. Boston, *A View of the Covenant of Grace from the Sacred Records* (Edinburgh, 1734), 30. Whitefield 1:51 of mine commends Boston's book and also speaks 2:233 of "the covenant of grace and redemption."

[295] E.g. *Complete Works*, 389 on his "covenant-office," and 736 for the Spirit as a partner in the 'covenant of peace." There is an exception in the brief mention of the *pactum* without the Spirit in "Of the Several Dispensations of the Covenant of Grace," in Ella, *Augustus Montague Toplady*, 672.

[296] Trueman, *John Owen, Reformed Catholic, Renaissance Man*, 86-87. See *The Works of John Owen*, 10:178-179 and 19:77-96. Owen seems to have developed his understanding of the *pactum* between 1643 and 1647 while working on his classic book on particular redemption *The Death of Death in the Death of Christ*.

[297] See W. J. Van Asselt, *The Federal Theology of Johannes Cocceius (1603-1669)* (Leiden: Brill, 2001), 233-234 who writes that for Cocceius, 'Apparently the Spirit is not a negotiating partner within the counsel of peace. The Spirit is certainly an active person in the implementation of the pact, but he is not a partner in the agreement itself.'

[298] See *The 'Miscellanies': 833-1152* ed. by A. Plantinga Pauw, in H. S. Stout ed., *The Works of Jonathan Edwards* (London: Yale University Press, 2002), No. 1062, 20:442.

[299] See W. Romaine, *A Treatise upon the Walk of Faith: Volume 1* (London, 1771), 21ff, 35, 49, 65, 104-105, 170, 222.

[300] J. Gill, *A Body of Doctrinal Divinity; or, a System of Evangelical Truths, Deduced from the Sacred Scriptures: Volume 1* (London, 1769), 394. On Gill's distinctive development of the *pactum* to include the Spirit, see R. A. Muller, "The Spirit and the Covenant: John Gill's Critique of the *Pactum Salutis*," *Foundations* 24 (1981): 4-14. Muller helpfully notes that Gill's motivation for including the Spirit in the eternal covenant was to preserve the idea of a totally gracious salvation provided for the elect and to protect against synergism, the idea that humans have to cooperate with the Spirit in the application of redemption (planned by Father and Son) to themselves. His doctrine rules out any disjunction between the eternal plan of God and its temporal execution.

writing, "Sweet Spirit of grace, Thy mercy we bless, For thy eminent share in the council of peace."[301]

Toplady wrote most fully on this subject in a discourse entitled "Clerical Subscription No Grievance: or, The doctrines of the Church of England proved to be the doctrines of Christ" (1772). There he declared that, "The covenant of grace and redemption which subsisted between the three divine persons, before all worlds, in behalf of the Church and people of God, held a distinguished place in that scheme of doctrine preached by the Lord from heaven."[302] He cites various biblical passages in support of this contention, including Luke 22:29 (in Greek) of which Witsius was so fond,[303] Hebrews 13:20, John 17:1-4 and 19:30, and Isaiah 48:16.[304] He also alludes in passing to the "counsel of peace" in Zechariah 6:13.[305] His immediate impulse after citing Scripture, however, is to demonstrate that this is a permissible and authentically *Anglican* doctrine: "Nor does our excellent establishment lose sight of this momentous article," he writes, citing Article 17, the *Te Deum*, the Communion Service, the Homily on the Nativity, the Second Homily on the Passion, and the Homily on the Resurrection to establish this.[306] My purpose is not to prove he is right to find the covenant of redemption alluded to in the Anglican formularies,

---

301 *Complete Works*, 909 (verse 4). "Council of peace" echoes Zechariah 6:13, a verse often cited in connection with the eternal covenant. The *Gospel Magazine* version of this hymn in Ella, *Augustus Montague Toplady*, 432 also contains the verse to Christ, "With joy we've beheld / Our sentence repeal'd / And sing thy Eternal Engagements fulfill'd."

302 *Complete Works*, 344-345.

303 H. Witsius, *The Economy of the Covenants Between God and Man: Comprehending a Complete Body of Divinity* Volume 1 (London: R. Baynes, 1822), 166-167. See also J. M. Beach, "The Doctrine of the *Pactum Salutis*," especially 122.

304 Gill, *A Body of Doctrinal Divinity: Volume 1*, 394 also cites this text as supportive of the Spirit's participation in the *pactum*. The text of the Hebrew (and LXX) here is not conclusive but has traditionally (see KJV) been taken to refer to the Spirit sending Christ, reading רוח (*ruach*, Spirit) as subject rather than object. In the middle ages, Peter Lombard, *The Sentences. Book 1: The Mystery of the Trinity* trans. G. Silano (Toronto: Pontifical Institute of Mediaeval Studies, 2007), 79 (1.15.3) takes this reading, corroborated by the use of Isaiah 61:1-2 in Luke 4:18-19, and attributes it to early church fathers Ambrose and Augustine. He sees no contradiction between this sending of the Son by the Spirit and the *filioque* clause of the creed, which he fully endorses, saying that the sending of the Son into the world, "is the joint work of the Father and Son and Holy Spirit" (81).

305 Regarding the controversial use of Zechariah 6:13 in this regard and on the importance for this doctrine of reading the Bible in the original languages (especially Luke 22:29) see R. A. Muller, "Toward the *Pactum Salutis:* Locating the Origins of a Concept," *Mid-America Journal of Theology* 18 (2007), 37-41.

306 *Complete Works*, 344-345.

but merely to point to the fact that Toplady was keen to demonstrate that distinctively Reformed doctrine has solid Anglican credentials as well as a basis in Scripture.

We have, therefore, identified Augustus Montague Toplady as Evangelical, as Reformed, and as an Anglican. This will help us considerably as we consider now the fourth part of his identity as a Reformed Evangelical Anglican controversialist.

5. Augustus Montague Toplady: Defender of 'Mercy Alone'

The envy, malice, and fury of Wesley's party are inconceivable. But, violently as they hate me, I dare not, I cannot, hate them in return. I have not so learned Christ. They have my prayers and my best wishes for their present and eternal salvation. But their errors have my opposition also.

- Toplady to Ryland (30th April 1773)

Toplady's first publication was a book of poems on sacred subjects, and it is clear he had a natural talent for verse which has justly earned him enduring fame as a hymn writer.[307] His second publication, however, was a work of controversy, the first of many such volumes to flow from his busy pen in the last 10 years of his short life. At the same time as Captain James Cook was mapping out the boundaries of the vast Pacific Ocean, Toplady was outlining and re-emphasising the legitimate boundaries of Anglican and Evangelical doctrine. In his many exchanges with Arminian opponents in the wake of that opening salvo he proved himself to be a Reformed Evangelical Anglican apologist of the first rank. In this chapter we will examine his major doctrinal and historical emphases as they develop over the course of his career as a defender of the faith. As we unpack his polemics we will see that the heartbeat of his writing is not to defend an esoteric or narrow system of theology, but to protect and guard the gospel of grace and the Church of England as a place where that gospel of salvation by God's mercy alone can thrive.

In the immediate background to Toplady's engagements there had been earlier battles in the ongoing war between Calvinists and Arminians in which the familiar trenches had been dug and battle lines drawn up. For example Daniel Whitby (1637-1726) had thrown down the gauntlet with his *Discourse on the True Import of the Words Election and Reprobation,* in which he dismisses Reformed views of the imputation of Adam's sin, election, and definite atonement.[308] It was in response to this

[307] A. M. Toplady, *Poems on Sacred Subjects* (Dublin, 1759).

[308] D. Whitby, *Discourse on the True Import of the Words Election and Reprobation* (London, 1710).

that Toplady's friend John Gill (1697-1771) had written perhaps his most famous work, *The Cause of God and Truth*,[309] and others such as the Congregationalist Thomas Ridgley (1667-1734) also weighed in to the debate.[310]

After the cleavage between Wesley and Whitefield over these same issues from 1738 onwards, the next major milepost in the controversy was when James Hervey of Weston Favell entered the lists with his book *Theron and Aspasio*.[311] This featured a dialogue between two fictional characters concerning "the most important and interesting subjects" the subtitle stated, including Scripture, the Fall, and the Atonement; but what he called "the grand article" was "the imputed righteousness of our divine Lord."[312] This sparked what is sometimes referred to as the second Calvinist controversy (the first being the cold war between Wesley and Whitefield in the 1740s). Wesley and others such as his Swiss Arminian friend the Revd. J. Fletcher (of Madeley) attacked Hervey,[313] because as J. C. Ryle says, "Hundreds were reached by Hervey's writings, who would never have condescended to listen to Whitefield's voice... *Theron and Aspasio* met with acceptance all over England and Scotland, and obliged even worldly critics to take notice of it."[314] Hervey responded gently to Wesley,[315] but a bitter correspondence ensued when others also chimed in to defend Hervey,[316] though Wesley paid him the compliment of imitating

---

[309] J. Gill, *The Cause of God and Truth* 4 Parts (London, 1735–8). Toplady records reading "Gill against Wesley" on predestination in 1767, in *Complete Works*, 4, which may be a reference to Gill's *The Doctrine of Predestination Stated, and Set in the Scripture Light* (London, 1752), on which see R. W. Oliver, "John Gill (1697-1771): His Life and Ministry" in M. A. G. Haykin (ed.), *The Life and Thought of John Gill (1697-1771): A Tercentennial Appreciation* (Leiden: Brill, 1997), 28-30.

[310] T. Ridgley, *A Body of Divinity* (London, 1731).

[311] J. Hervey, *Theron and Aspasio* (London, 1755).

[312] From the Preface.

[313] See Wesley's *Preservative Against Unsettled Notions in Religion* (Bristol, 1758) noted in T. Jackson (ed.), *The Works of John Wesley* (Grand Rapids: Baker, 2007), 14:239 and also his "Preface to a Treatise on Justification Extracted from Mr. John Goodwin wherein all that is personal, in letters just published, under the name of the Rev. Mr. Hervey, is answered," in 10:316-346.

[314] J. C. Ryle, *Christian Leaders of the Eighteenth Century* (Edinburgh: Banner of Truth), 339 342.

[315] See J. Hervey, *Aspasio Vindicated in Eleven Letters from Mr. Hervey to the Rev. John Wesley* (London, 1764).

[316] See *A Sufficient Answer to "Letters to the Author of 'Theron and Aspasio.'" In a Letter to the Author* in *The Works of John Wesley*, 10:298-306 and *Some Remarks on 'A Defence of the Preface to the Edinburgh edition of Aspasio Vindicated,'* in 10:346-357.

his dialogue style in presentations of his own Evangelical Arminianism.[317]

Toplady was clearly on the side of Hervey; as his journals testify, he was reading "dear Mr. Hervey," "excellent Hervey," "the seraphic Mr. Hervey" at an early stage.[318] The entry in his diary for July 30th 1760 is remarkable for a mere 19 year old, but not unusual for him: "Read the Greek Testament and Hervey for several hours this morning," — and this before breakfast. Over the course of his own career as a controversialist, Toplady also caused several other works by Hervey to be published.[319] As has been rightly said, however, Toplady himself was, "the ablest of all who wrote on the Calvinist side... a far abler and far more deeply read man than Hervey."[320] To his contribution we now turn.

5.1. *The Church of England Vindicated from the Charge of Arminianism (1769)*

Toplady's personal involvement in what are possibly better known as the Arminian Controversies began when in 1769 he came to the defence of six undergraduates (unknown to him personally),[321] who had been expelled from St. Edmund Hall, Oxford the previous year. The judgment against them was perhaps partly motivated by their lower-class upbringing and partly by their youthful over-confidence,[322] but more specifically, the Vice Chancellor stated, they had committed the horrid crime of attending a prayer meeting:

---

[317] See e.g. "A Dialogue between a Predestinarian and his Friend," and "A Dialogue between an Antinomian and his Friend," in *The Works of John Wesley*, 10:259-276.

[318] G. M. Ella, *Augustus Montague Toplady: A Debtor to Mercy Alone* (Eggleston, Durham: Go Publications, 2000), 402, 411-414 and *Complete Works*, 5.

[319] See the list in T. Wright, *Augustus M. Toplady and Contemporary Hymn-writers* (London: Farncombe and Son, 1911), 292. On Toplady's love for Hervey see Ella, *Augustus Montage Toplady*, 128-133.

[320] C. J. Abbey and J. H. Overton, *The English Church in the Eighteenth Century* (London: Longmans, Green, and Co, 1887), 362, 365. C. Sydney Carter, *The English Church in the Eighteenth Century* (London: Church Book Room Press, 1948), 75 also calls him the most able.

[321] *Complete Works*, 662. Five letters from John Newton to Thomas Jones, one of the six students, can be found in J. Newton, *Cardiphonia, or The Utterance of the Heart* (Edinburgh: Waugh and Innes, 1824), 282-296. Wright, *The Life of Augustus M. Toplady*, 73 identifies these letters as to Jones.

[322] In one of Newton's letters to Thomas Jones (*Cardiphonia*, 294) he says, "Your friends here have thought you at times harsh and hasty in your manner, and rather inclining to self-confidence."

> It having also appeared to me that Benjamin Kay, of the said Hall, by his own confession, had frequented illicit conventicles in a private house in this town, where he had heard extempore prayers frequently offered up by one Hewitt, a staymaker. Moreover, it having been proved by sufficient evidence that he held methodistical principles, viz., 'the doctrine of absolute election; that the spirit of God works irresistibly, that once a child of God always a child of God.' That he had endeavoured to instil the same principles into others and exhorted them to continue steadfastly in them against all opposition. — Therefore, I, D. Durell, by virtue, etc., do expel the said Benjamin Kay from the said Hall, and hereby pronounce him also expelled.[323]

Several leading Evangelicals leapt to the defence of the undergraduates who were thus promoting Evangelical Calvinism.[324] George Whitefield, described the expelled as "entire friends to the doctrines and liturgy of our Church," and wondered at "so severe a sentence, in an age when almost every kind of proper discipline is held with so lax a rein."[325] Richard Hill wrote a defence of the students and their "methodistical principles," called *Pietas Oxoniensis*, to which the public orator of the University, Revd. Dr. Nowell, felt constrained to reply, attempting in the process to assert that the Church of England's doctrine was properly Arminian. It was this public reply by Nowell to Hill which provoked Toplady himself into the ring with his first major controversial work, *The Church of England Vindicated from the Charge of Arminianism.*

Toplady's avowed aim in this book of about 150 pages in length is to show that regardless of whether the Reformed view of the gospel is biblically correct or not it remains nevertheless the official doctrine of the Church of England. His purpose in demonstrating this, of course, is to suggest that non-Calvinist subscription to the Anglican formularies is hypocritical and insincere, and therefore that it was not Benjamin Kay and his friends who ought to have been expelled from the university (where

---

[323] For this and the similar judgments against the other students see W. Gibson, *Religion and Society in England and Wales 1689-1800* Documents in Early Modern Social History (London: Leicester University Press, 1998), 127-129.

[324] It is clear throughout Newton's correspondence with Thomas Jones that the young man had a distaste for Arminianism and shared Newton's Calvinist sentiments, though reading between the lines he may have been somewhat more combative about them than his mentor.

[325] See *The Works of the Reverend George Whitefield: Volume IV* (London: 1771), 314.

subscription was required by all students and tutors). His method of approach is two-fold. He begins with a historical survey of the Church of England's establishment in the times of Edward VI and Elizabeth I down to the Synod of Dort and beyond, and then proceeds to a doctrinal examination of the formularies themselves — Articles, Catechism, Liturgy, and Homilies.

Throughout this material Toplady constantly draws two very important links, in order to prove guilt by association or guilt by tendency: Arminianism bears a striking resemblance to the earlier heresy of Pelagianism, and it also tends towards Roman Catholicism. So, for example he quotes a learned scholar who outlines the ancient arch-heretic's theological scheme thus: "The cause of predestination to grace and glory was the foresight of good works, and of perseverance therein, resulting from a right use of our free-will: and that there is no such thing as predestination unto death." Toplady then concludes, "That these are the doctrines of the Arminians now, as they were of Pelagius then, needs no proof."[326] John Wesley indeed was happy to identify with Pelagius who he saw as a true Christian, a holy man, and part of the righteous remnant in church history, unfairly stigmatized as a heretic by an angry and abusive Augustine who was not worth listening to. "I verily believe," he mordantly declared, "the real heresy of Pelagius was neither more nor less than this: The holding that Christians may, by the grace of God, (not without it; that I take to be a mere slander,) 'go on to perfection;' or, in other words, 'fulfil the law of Christ.'"[327]

Toplady also linked Arminianism with Rome, averring that "The Arminian tenets belong to the church of Rome. Her's they are, and to her they should be returned. From her they came, and to her they lead."[328] He returns to this connection at the end of the work, saying, "Calvinism is the religion of England, and... Arminianism is the heresy of Rome." Not that all Arminians are fond of 'Popery' as such but "Arminianism is the forerunner which prepares the way for Rome, and, if not discarded in time, will one day open the door to it."[329]

J. C. Ryle seems to consider Toplady's identification of Arminians

---

[326] *Complete Works*, 612. See also 623 for the description of Arminius as "Pelagius the second." He is, of course, also aware of differences between Pelagius and Arminius, *Complete Works*, 724.

[327] *The Works of John Wesley* 6:328-329.

[328] *Complete Works*, 614.

[329] *Complete Works*, 661-662.

with Pelagians and Papists a scandalous outrage.[330] Yet these were, of course, not unusual connections to make at this time. Whitefield, Gill, and many others also drew attention to the theological links,[331] and it had been standard practice in the seventeenth century debates against Laudianism and the Remonstrants too, books being published with names like *A parallel: of new-old Pelgiarminian error* and *Pelagius redivivus: or Pelagius raked out of the ashes by Arminius and his schollers* (these both by Daniel Featley in 1626).[332] John Owen's first publication in 1642 was called *A Display of Arminianism: Being a Discovery of the Old Pelagian Idol, Free Will, with the New Goddess Contingency, Advancing Themselves into the Throne of the God of Heaven, to the Prejudice of his Grace.*[333] It was also not unusual when elsewhere Toplady linked the rise of immorality in the country with the rise of Arminianism in the Church.[334] Besides, Sellon, Wesley, and other Arminians accused Calvinists of all manner of evils, alleging they were unchristian, heretical, Islamic, fatalistic, cold and emotionless sloths whose principles proved they must be uninterested in evangelism and such like. So accusing them of a tendency to Pelagianism (an identification Wesley appeared happily to accept) hardly seems comparable on the insult scale.

On the historical front, Toplady lays the blame for much of the latitudinarian approach to doctrine at the feet of Bishop Burnet's exposition of the Thirty-nine Articles. This classic and influential 1699 commentary on the confessional basis of the established church has been seen by some as setting the seal on the new post-Restoration Arminian

---

[330] Ryle, *Christian Leaders*, 380.

[331] On Gill see T. J. Nettles, "John Gill and the Evangelical Awakening," in M. A. G. Haykin (ed.), *The Life and Thought of John Gill*, 138-139 and on Whitefield see L. Gatiss (ed.), *The Sermons of George Whitefield: Part 1* (Watford: Church Society, 2010), 263, 267, 274 and *Select Sermons of George Whitefield* (Edinburgh: Banner of Truth, 1958), 116, 121, 129 where he calls Arminianism "antichristian" and "the back way to Popery."

[332] See also A. Milton, *Catholic and Reformed: The Roman and Protestant Churches in English Protestant Thought, 1600-1640* (Cambridge: Cambridge University Press, 2002), 418 on this equation being made by "English moderate Calvinists."

[333] See W. H. Goold (ed.), *The Works of John Owen* (Edinburgh: Hunter and Johnstone, 1850-1853), 10:6 where he speaks of the "new popish-arminian errors" of the "Belgic semi-Pelagians" influencing the Church, and also 3:245 where he says, "we plead for nothing but the known doctrine of the ancient catholic church, declared in the writings of the most learned fathers and determinations of councils against the Pelagians, whose errors and heresies are again revived among us by a crew of Socinianized Arminians."

[334] E.g. *Complete Works*, 278, 759.

dispensation,[335] and by others as indicative of the continuing strength of Reformed views in a majority Arminian church.[336] It may be true that his discussion of the Reformed position on disputed points shows it remained a viable and vibrant option, but what is clear is that Burnet's approach fostered a studied ambiguity and a less-than-straightforward subscription to the Articles. While not entirely negative about Burnet's "masterly performance," Toplady wrote that "Burnet plays fast and loose whenever Calvinism and subscription fall in his way." He quoted a long passage from John Edwards' *Veritas Redux* which accuses Burnet of making the Articles "dark and ambiguous" in places and of fostering dissimulation, equivocation, and lack of integrity in the clergy.[337] He also notes that the Convocation of 1701 severely censured Burnet's exposition for precisely this reason.

Toplady's vindication of the Church includes a glancing blow at a future foe, John Wesley, for his approach to the Articles which, Wesley had claimed, merely define terms rather than affirm doctrine.[338] Yet Toplady reserves particular scorn for the historical revisionism of Peter Heylyn who attempted "the most laboured effort ever yet made to father Arminianism on the Church of England," especially since Nowell appeared to have relied heavily on Heylyn's polemical pattern and sources.[339] The Articles were not written to allow a diversity of opinion on foundational issues but to remove such diversity (as the preface to the Articles itself states) and establish agreement in Reformed fundamentals.[340] "Were the same insincerity and prevarications allowed of in the secular affairs of common life, which too often obtain in religious transactions, all social connections would quickly be at an end, and every band by which mankind are tied to each other must vanish as a wreath of smoke," Toplady concluded.[341] After his historical tour-de-force in which he proves everyone of importance in the English Reformation to have

---

[335] N. Tyacke, "Religious controversy during the seventeenth century: the case of Oxford," in *Aspects of English Protestantism c. 1530-1700* (Manchester: Manchester University Press, 2001), 307.

[336] S. Hampton, *Anti-Arminians: The Anglican Reformed Tradition from Charles II to George I* (Oxford: Oxford University Press, 2008), 271.

[337] *Complete Works*, 617.

[338] *Complete Works*, 615-616.

[339] *Complete Works*, 620, 624-625, 633.

[340] *Complete Works*, 620.

[341] *Complete Works*, 621.

been Reformed (even Shakespeare was a Calvinist, he declares),[342] Toplady traces this line of doctrinal descent through the Lambeth Articles, the Synod of Dort, and the Post-Restoration Reformed Anglican divines.

Turning to a doctrinal examination of the Anglican formularies, Toplady focuses particularly on what they teach concerning predestination, the intent of the atonement, total inability, invincible grace, justification by faith alone, and the influence and indwelling of the Holy Spirit. Apart from the last, these are the common sticking points in the Arminian controversies. His focus on the Spirit was no doubt motivated by the Vice Chancellor of Oxford's identification of the expelled students' doctrine of the Spirit as particularly "methodistical"; as we have noted before, Whitefield claimed that, "As soon as a person begins to talk of the work of the Holy Ghost, they cry, you are a Methodist."[343] As Michael Haykin has said, "Revival went hand in hand with a quickened interest in pneumatology."[344]

On election, Toplady is at pains to show logically how election to life in Article 17 must also imply the negative idea of preterition or reprobation. The original Forty-two Articles of 1553 included the phrase "the decrees of predestination" (plural), which makes this point somewhat clearer.[345] Although Toplady confesses that this is not so obvious in the authoritative Thirty-nine Articles, reprobation is however spoken of unambiguously in the Homilies.[346] Saying that reprobation is not explicitly asserted in Article 17 does not, however, mean the thought is absent, as

---

342 *Complete Works*, 635. Today, even a more subtle attempt to show him as a *Christian* writer can raise a few eyebrows: L. Ryken, "Shakespeare as a Christian Writer," in *Reformation 21* (June 2009).

343 *Eighteen Sermons Preached by the late Rev. George Whitefield A.M.* (London, 1771), 381-382.

344 M. Haykin, "'The Sum of All Good': John Ryland, Jr. and the Doctrine of the Holy Spirit," *Churchman* 103/4 (1989), 333.

345 See G. Bray (ed.), *Documents of the English Reformation* (Cambridge: James Clarke and Co, 1994), 295.

346 *Complete Works*, 646-648, 652. He cites two Homilies, for example, as revealing the underlying assumptions of the English Reformers concerning reprobation. Homily 22, "An Information of them which take Offence at certain Places of Holy Scripture," Part 2, says, "Christ Jesus is a fall to the reprobate, which yet perish through their own default; so is his word, yea, the whole book of God, a cause of damnation unto them." In addition to this, Homily 29, "An Homily for Rogation-Week," Part 1, says of God that, "he may do what liketh him, and none can resist him. For he worketh all things in his secret judgment to his own pleasure, yea, even the wicked to damnation," alluding to Proverbs 16:4.

some suggest.[347] Toplady notes that when Article 17 speaks of "the sentence of God's predestination" being a cause of desperation and reckless ungodliness for those lacking the Spirit it cannot be referring to the positive aspect of 'predestination to glory,' since why would desperation follow if one considered oneself chosen for that? Indeed, the Article states that a godly consideration of predestination is, "full of sweet, pleasant, and unspeakable comfort." It must therefore relate to the negative aspect of the decree, i.e. God's sentence (that word itself implying a negative judgment) of preterition, rejection, or reprobation by which the un-elect, considered as fallen in Adam, are passed by with respect to salvation, left in sin, and therefore destined for stumbling disobedience (1 Peter 2:8). He is content to say this is implied by the predestination of believers to life as asserted in the rest of the Article,[348] but the Article also here "plainly speaks of two distinct sorts or persons; the elect, and the non-elect,"[349] with the saving decree of God's mercy or the damning sentence of God's justice determinative for each.

For Toplady it was clear that what the Article teaches is that supposed reprobation cannot be used as an excuse for immorality, not that there is no such thing as reprobation. This reading is confirmed by a passage in Cranmer's proposed canon law reform, the *Reformatio Legum Ecclesiasticarum* where he writes,

> On the fringe of the church there are many who live in a wild and dissolute way, who when they get interested in the subject, being dissipated by excess and completely cut off from the Spirit of Christ, always toss predestination and rejection, or (as they usually call it), reprobation, into their speech, arguing that since God by his eternal counsel has already determined something, both

[347] W. H. Griffith Thomas, *The Principles of Theology: An Introduction to the Thirty-nine Articles* (London: Vine Books, 1930), 238 claims "there is no reference to anything else" other than predestination to life in this Article and (244) that reprobation and preterition are not a part of Church of England doctrine. This is often repeated by others such as R. Burrows, *John Wesley in the Reformation Tradition: The Protestant and Puritan Nature of Methodism Rediscovered* (Stoke-on-Trent: Tentmaker, 2009), 32. This view ignores the evidence of the Homilies cited by Toplady and is at odds with the observation of J. L. Schwenk, *Catholic Spirit: Wesley, Whitefield, and the Quest for Evangelical Unity in Eighteenth-Century British Methodism* (Plymouth: Scarecrow Press, 2008), 28 who says "The Article makes a strong statement concerning 'predestination to eternal life,' and an underlying, yet evident appeal for reprobation."

[348] Toplady quotes the Arminian apologist Peter Heylyn himself to the effect that predestination to life must imply an opposite dereliction, *Complete Works*, 192 note y.

[349] *Complete Works*, 647.

> concerning salvation and destruction, they have some excuse for their wrongdoings and crimes and all manner of evil. And when pastors upbraid their dissipated and disgraceful life, they blame God's will for their crimes and by that defence consider that the reprimands of admonitions are wasted... Wherefore everyone must be warned by us that in undertaking actions they should not rely on the decrees of predestination, but adapt their entire way of life to the laws of God, and contemplate that both promises to the good as well as threats to the bad are generally set forth to him in the Holy Scriptures.[350]

In other words, one may be reprobate but one is not to assume this in deciding how to live, since "the decrees of predestination are unknown to us," as the 1553 edition of Article 17 says. Rather, we are to obey the warnings of Scripture and trust the promises. As Article 17 says, "in our doings, that Will of God is to be followed, which we have expressly declared to us in the Word of God." So we are not to base our rejection of God on a presumption that he has not chosen us. Scripture, when it speaks of reprobation, does not apply it in this manner. Whitefield had claimed Burnet himself in support of his belief in reprobation from Article 17.[351] Burnet asserts that there is no mention or hint of reprobation in the Article, though he does however say, "the Calvinists have less occasion for scruple since the Article does seem more plainly to favour them," pointing particularly to the line about "the sentence of God's predestination" as not fitting the Arminian hypothesis and reading.[352] This was at the heart of Toplady's contention against Nowell's attack on the excluded Evangelical students from Oxford.

The intent of the atonement is usually connected in Toplady's thought with election. So it is here. If election is limited to a certain number, he says, then "a limited redemption necessarily follows; unless you will suppose that, in the judgment of the Church, the will of God the Father and the will of God the Redeemer were discordant, and that the

---

[350] See G. Bray (ed.), *Tudor Church Reform: The Henrician Canons of 1535 and the* Reformatio Legum Ecclesiasticarum (Woodbridge, Suffolk: Boydell Press, 2000) Church of England Record Society Volume 8, 211-213. I have slightly altered the translation to make it more readable. See also Sermon 40 on John 16:8 (Vol 2, 172-173 of my doc) for Whitefield addressing someone who misused the doctrine of reprobation in the way foreseen by Article 17 and the *Reformatio Legum Ecclesiasticarum.*

[351] *George Whitefield's Journals* (Edinburgh: Banner of Truth, 1960), 575.

[352] G. Burnet, *An Exposition of the Thirty-nine Articles of the Church of England* (London, 1699), 168.

latter exceeded his commission by dying for more than the former gave him in charge to save."[353] This he cannot countenance, praising Christ in his hymn *The Method of Salvation* by saying, "Great Surety of thine, Thou didst not decline To concur with the Father's most gracious design," and "Father, Spirit, and Son, Agree thus in One, The salvation of those he has mark'd for his own."[354]

He also spends some time examining the Homilies to show that they speak of the cross having saved a particular group ("them that are sanctified," God's people) concluding that, "in the opinion of our Church, Christ did not lay down his life, to put men into a salvable state, and render their salvation barely possible [the Arminian view]; but actually and absolutely secured the discharge of those redeemed, and, indeed, it would have been no redemption without this." It was a definite, efficacious atonement rather than a general, universal atonement, unlimited in scope but entirely limited in efficacy. Therefore it cannot be said that those who are condemned at the last day (the reprobate) have had their debt paid by Christ on the cross, for is it not inconsistent with justice "that God the Father should demand double payment of the self-same debts, by charging sin first to the Surety's account and then the sinner's afterwards?"[355] This idea Toplady also put into poetic form in his hymn which begins "From Whence This Fear and Unbelief," writing,

> If thou hast my Discharge procur'd,
> And freely in my Room endur'd
> The whole of Wrath Divine:
> Payment God cannot twice demand,
> First at my bleeding Surety's hand,
> And then again at mine.[356]

Moreover, he suggests, if penal substitutionary atonement is correct (as the Church of England affirms) then the result could only be either universal salvation or particular redemption. Since universal salvation is not the Anglican position (see especially Article 18), the only conclusion must be that atonement/redemption is co-extensive with election.[357] In

---

[353] *Complete Works*, 626.
[354] *Complete Works*, 909.
[355] *Complete Works*, 653.
[356] A. M. Toplady, *Hymns and Sacred Poems on a Variety of Divine Subjects* (London: Daniel Sedgwick, 1860), 155. The title of the hymn is *Faith reviving*.
[357] For this same logic see S. Jeffery, M. Ovey, A. Sach, *Pierced for our Transgressions: Rediscovering the Glory of Penal Substitution* (Leicester: IVP, 2007), 268-278.

addition, Christ "cannot be said to have purchased salvation for any, for whom he did not likewise obtain those influences of saving grace without which final salvation cannot be had."[358] In other words, if he bought salvation for all why is the gift of faith not also purchased for all and given to all? Or, to look at it a different way, is the sin of unbelief not atoned for in the supposedly universal atonement pleaded for by Arminians? Toplady also finds it difficult to believe that an omniscient God would pay an infinite price while leaving it uncertain as to whether the purchased blessing would be enjoyed by those for whom it was bought. Surely if God foreknows all then he would have planned better and not propounded "absurd doctrines of a random salvation, and of redemption without a plan."[359] In this way, of course, the definite plan of God in the eternal agreement between Father, Son, and Spirit is intimately connected to the particular redemption made by the Son for those given to him (John 10:29, 17:24).

Nowell had tried to use the *Te Deum* in the Prayer Book which says to Christ, "thou didst open the kingdom of heaven to all believers" to establish the universal scope of the atonement. Toplady concludes from that same text, however, that all it proves is that "in the judgment of the Church they alone were intentionally redeemed by Christ who should finally believe."[360] Toplady by no means denies the sufficient value, "availableness," or intrinsic sufficiency of the cross; yet he is careful to make a distinction to say "intrinsic sufficiency is one thing; intentional and actual efficacy is another."[361] His final major argument from the Homilies is from the way they teach that the believer may say with the apostle Paul "he loved me and gave himself for me" (in the Homily on the Sacrament). So, he says, "if Christ loved all men, and gave himself for every individual of mankind, he must of course have loved me and gave himself for me: consequently, this assured faith of his being my lover, my sacrifice, and my Saviour in particular, could not, upon the principle of universal redemption, be so high and distinguishing a privilege as the

---

[358] *Complete Works,* 653.

[359] *Complete Works,* 648.

[360] *Complete Works,* 641. See also 643-644.

[361] *Complete Works,* 653 note r. Peter Lombard, *The Sentences. Book 3: On the Incarnation of the Word* trans. G. Silano (Toronto: Pontifical Institute for Mediaeval Studies, 2008), 86 (3.20.5.1) classically states this formula, "He offered himself on the altar of the cross not to the devil, but to the triune God, and he did so for all with regard to the sufficiency of the price, but only for the elect with regard to its efficacy, because he brought about salvation only for the predestined."

homily here presents it."[362] The idea of Christ's personal atonement for "me" in Galatians 2:20 becomes entirely impersonal if universalised, and the cross is thus evacuated of any especial importance in assuring the believer, who may turn elsewhere for assurance instead (such as to their works or experience) rather than to the particular love of God to his people as demonstrated at the cross.

Nowell had brought up the fact that at the Synod of Dort the British delegate John Hales apparently "bid John Calvin good night." He also claimed that "our English divines who attended the synod began to have less reverence for the doctrines of Calvin."[363] This misrepresented Hales, of course, who if he ever truly moved away from Calvin that night was certainly reconciled to him the very next morning, since his subsequent writing affirms doctrines such as election and reprobation as firmly as any other Calvinist.[364] Perhaps, however, Nowell was alluding to the hypothetical universalism of the British delegates,[365] which has been seen by some as a softening of Reformed theology in an attempt to unite anti-Arminians under pressure at the start of the seventeenth century and lessen opposition to Reformed doctrine.[366] Though Toplady may well be aware of the nuances in this debate, they did not matter for his main purpose. Hales, Davenant (who Toplady styles "this learned and evangelical prelate"),[367] and the other British delegates to Dort remained staunchly Calvinist even if they wanted to stress some conditional and universal aspects to redemption as well as a particularistic scheme. They happily signed the firmly anti-Arminian Canons of Dort which were carefully framed so as not to exclude their non-Bezan strain of Reformed doctrine.[368] They therefore stood opposed to the Arminianism of Nowell and others; Toplady even quotes Davenant elsewhere in favour of absolute

---

[362] *Complete Works*, 654.

[363] *Complete Works*, 634.

[364] *Complete Works*, 634-635. See also W. R. Godfrey, "John Hales' Good-Night to John Calvin," in C. R. Trueman and R. Scott Clark (eds.), *Protestant Scholasticism: Essays in Reassessment* (Milton Keynes: Paternoster, 1999), 165-180.

[365] Seen in G. Carleton et al, *The Collegiat Suffrage of the Divines of Great Britaine, concerning the five articles controverted in the Low Countries* (London, 1629), 47-48.

[366] See J. D. Moore, *English Hypothetical Universalism: John Preston and the Softening of Reformed Theology* (Cambridge: Eerdmans, 2007), 187-213.

[367] *Complete Works*, 714 note u.

[368] See my "Shades of opinion within a generic Calvinism: The Particular Redemption Debate at the Westminster Assembly," and "A Deceptive Clarity? Particular Redemption in the Westminster Standards," *Reformed Theological Review* (forthcoming, 2010).

predestination and reprobation.[369]

Toplady spends time defending the other doctrines under attack by the Arminians with a deft use of both the Articles and the Homilies of the Church of England. Near the end of his vindication he outlines several fatal consequences which have arisen because of the national church's departure from what he calls "the principles of the Reformation." These were that the Church and churchmen were "the scorn of infidels"; that the ordinary people of England were deplorably ignorant of the gospel; that the established churches were empty while dissenting Calvinist chapels were full because people were forced to go outside the national church "to hear the doctrines of their own Church preached"; English religion had become moralistic and deistic; the Church of England had become "a state-engine on the one hand, and a genteel trade on the other"; and Roman Catholicism had made alarming progress. To forsake Arminianism and return to the doctrines of the Reformation was the only way to tackle this malaise he said, adding:

> Whilst the Calvinistic doctrines were the language of our pulpits as well as of our articles, the Reformation made a swift and extensive progress. But ever since our articles and our pulpits have been at variance, the Reformation has been at a stand.[370]

I have spent so long outlining some of the main arguments in this, Toplady's first foray into controversy, because in it we see the general thrust and pattern of all his subsequent work in this area. *The Historic Proof of the Doctrinal Calvinism of the Church of England* may well be his *magnum opus*, but *The Church of England Vindicated from the Charge of Arminianism* is his signature book. It summarises his historical and doctrinal viewpoint in much shorter compass, demonstrates his masterful ability to marshal the official formularies of the Church for his position, and has a well-defined polemical thrust in wanting to recapture the Reformation's gospel of grace and salvation by 'mercy alone.' Naturally, he stands on the shoulders of those who had engaged in these debates previously and is able to deploy the best of their arguments in rhetorically effective ways at a key moment in the wider struggle. Yet he does it with such composure and aplomb that even those who may not find it entirely compelling would find it difficult not to admire this confident contribution from the 28 year old Vicar of Broad

[369] *Complete Works*, 226.
[370] *Complete Works*, 661.

Hembury.

As Wright said of this exchange, "If Toplady's blade is of the keenest steel, if he is pitiless in exposing the sophistries of a scholarly opponent, he is also persistently courteous to that opponent... It is the address of one cultured gentleman to another cultured gentleman."[371] He concludes the book, however, by reminding Nowell of one of his predecessors as public orator at Oxford, Dr. South, who "after having long been a zealous Arminian, sacrificed his prejudices, submitted to superior evidence, and boldly avowed those Calvinistic doctrines which once he laboured to destroy." He cheekily adds, "it can be no insult to Dr. Nowell to wish that he may go and do likewise."[372]

5.2. *A Caveat against Unsound Doctrines (1770)*

A year later Toplady published a sermon on 1 Timothy 1:10 preached in Bethnal Green and Blackfriars called *A Caveat Against Unsound Doctrines*. It was taken down in shorthand and Toplady himself transcribed it for the sake of publication a few months later, he tells us.[373] By this time his reputation as a Calvinist was growing,[374] and after several pages in which he faithfully attempts to expound the first chapter of 1 Timothy, he turns to consider by way of application some modern teachings which he considered "contrary to sound doctrine." He asked the congregations what they thought of eight points of current controversy: conditional election, the dignity of human nature after the Fall, conditional redemption, justification by works, uneffectual grace (*sic*), Antinomianism, sinless perfection, the impossibility of assurance, and the possibility of falling finally from a state of real grace. The new items here which were not previously tackled so prominently were antinomianism and sinless perfection. This indicates that the shadow of John Wesley was beginning to loom larger over Toplady, since 'antinomian' was the Methodist leader's favourite insult directed towards Calvinists and, as we have seen before, perfectionism was one of Wesley's distinctive rallying cries.

Conditional election is given the longest treatment at the head of Toplady's list of unsound doctrines. Leaning on Romans 11 and Article 17

[371] Wright, *The Life of Augustus M. Toplady*, 72.
[372] *Complete Works*, 663.
[373] *Complete Works*, 307.
[374] *Complete Works*, 311.

he shows how jarring conditional election (the idea that God's choice of us is based on something we do) is to Scripture and to the formularies. His main interest is to show that a conditional election, based on God foreseeing our faith and works, ultimately hangs salvation on our sanctification rather than on God's sovereign grace, "the everlasting purpose of God," as Article 17 puts it. It therefore undercuts the gospel call of salvation through God's mercy alone. Unconditional election therefore takes its place at the head of Toplady's *ordo salutis*, which he derives from Article 17 and states as: "1. Election; 2. Effectual calling; 3. Apprehensive justification; 4. Manifestive adoption; 5. Sanctification; 6. Religious walking in good works; 7. Continuance in these to the end." Without such election it seems that people are only "saved by random, and without design," and a deity without a "determinate plan" in such an important matter was blasphemous and inconceivable.[375] Rather, God set his mark on a fixed group, the church: the Father loved it, the Son became a man of sorrows for it, and the Spirit cultivated and built it. Such grace does not destroy good works, however, since (as Ephesians 1:4 shows) "holiness is, itself, one end of election."[376]

Conditional redemption (or 'unlimited atonement') is given a longer treatment, after election, than any other "unsound" doctrine identified in the sermon. Again, he seeks to show how the Arminian idea that the death of Christ only puts humanity into a 'salvable state' but does not actually save anybody for definite unless they fulfil certain conditions, undermines salvation by grace alone. On this scheme, he says, "the adorable Mediator... is represented as bequeathing to [us] only a few spiritual lottery-tickets, which may come up, blanks or prizes, just as the wheel of chance and human caprice happens to turn... The Messiah's obedience and sufferings stand, it seems, for mere cyphers; until our own free-will is so kind as to... render them of value." Moreover, this turns Christ "into a spiritual huckster, who, having purchased certain blessings of his Father, sells them out afterwards to men upon terms and conditions!"[377] These are powerful new rhetorical methods of presenting the same doctrine he had outlined previously in 1769, though he cites some of the same texts (such as Hebrews 10:14) in support. He also uses similar expressions to describe the alternative as "a random redemption, and a precarious salvation," while showing that Paul's inference in

---

[375] *Complete Works*, 313.
[376] *Complete Works*, 314. He also quotes 2 Thess 2:13 and 1 Thess 5:8-9 here.
[377] *Complete Works*, 315.

Romans 8:34 that no-one can condemn those for whom Christ died is overthrown by the Arminian hypothesis which claims that "millions of those for whom Christ died will be condemned."[378]

Toplady has framed the question here in terms of the effectiveness of the atonement, the conditionality of redemption, and God's intent. This enables him to use even John 1:29 ("the lamb of God who takes away the sin of the world"), a text sometimes used against limited atonement, in support of his doctrine of unconditional redemption. What Christ does is effective and actually takes away sin, as the verse says; it does not render sin forgivable upon certain human conditions which must be added to make it effective, as if (so to speak) God helps those who help themselves. If the question is framed in terms of the *extent* of the atonement alone, this text would seem to be a difficult one for a Calvinist. Yet Toplady skilfully undermines that narrowing of focus and puts the issue into a wider theological perspective, linking it very effectively with the gratuitous nature of salvation.

In pursuit of this goal, Toplady can also cite Article 31 in support of his doctrine because it speaks of an accomplished and finished work of Christ:

> The offering of Christ once made is that perfect redemption, propitiation, and satisfaction for all the sins of the whole world, both original and actual; and there is none other satisfaction for sin, but that alone. Wherefore the sacrifices of masses, in the which it was commonly said that the priest did offer Christ for the quick and the dead, to have remission of pain or guilt, were blasphemous fables and dangerous deceits.

Some, Toplady was aware, stumbled at the clause of this Article which said Christ's propitiation was made "for all the sins of the whole world," thinking this supported the idea that Christ died for all indiscriminately and in the same sense.[379] Wesley himself sometimes referred to this Article as being in his favour.[380] Yet this could not imply unlimited

---

[378] *Complete Works*, 316.

[379] For a modern example of such stumbling see T. L. Miethe, "The Universal Power of the Atonement," in C. H. Pinnock (ed), *The Grace of God, The Will of Man: A Case for Arminianism* (Grand Rapids: Academie, 1989), 88 and the withering response of J. I. Packer, "The Love of God: Universal and Particular," in T. R. Schreiner and B. A. Ware (eds.), *Still Sovereign: Contemporary Perspectives on Election, Foreknowledge, and Grace* (Grand Rapids: Baker, 2000), 289.

[380] *The Works of John Wesley*, 10:356, 383.

atonement any more than it meant unlimited salvation, says Toplady. He also shows from a comparative study of the Bible's own use of the word "world," that this allusion to 1 John 2:2 can refer ultimately to "a world within a world," such as the elect.[381] He might also have circumvented such objections, of course, by pointing out that the thrust and context of the Article is clearly the complete sufficiency of Christ's sacrifice contrary to the Roman doctrine of the Mass, and not about the extent of the atonement.[382] This is probably why there is no discussion of the extent of the atonement with regard to Article 31 in any of the standard commentaries on the Articles.[383] Even those scholarly commentators who dislike limited atonement realise that they cannot adequately make use of Article 31 against it,[384] since its purpose was to oppose the Mass and not to

[381] From Romans 1:8, 1 John 5:19, Revelation 12:9, 13:3 he shows that "world" in Scripture sometimes refers to a circumscribed group (such as "the Christian or non-Christian world") and does not necessarily include every single individual on the planet.

[382] He could also have mentioned that the Article does not quote the negative assertion in 1 John 2:2 that Christ was a propitiation for our sins "*and not for ours only*..." which it surely would have done if attempting to establish the Arminian point about universal, unlimited atonement. This clause is also omitted from the quotation of 1 John 2:1-2 in the 'comfortable words' in the *Book of Common Prayer* Communion liturgy.

[383] See, for example, T. Rogers, *The Faith, Doctrine, and Religion, Professed, and Protected in the Realme of England, and Dominions of the Same Expressed in 39 Articles* (Cambridge, 1607); G. Burnet, *An Exposition of the XXXIX Articles*; W. Beveridge, *Ecclesia Anglicana Ecclesia Catholica: or, The Doctrine of the Church of England Consonant to Scripture, Reason, and Fathers: in a Discourse upon The Thirty-nine Articles* (Oxford: Oxford University Press, 1846); E. H. Browne, *An Exposition of the Thirty-nine Articles of Religion: Historical and Doctrinal* (H. B. Durand: New York, 1865); A. P. Forbes, *An Explanation of the Thirty-nine Articles* (London: James Parker and Co, 1871); T. P. Boultbee, *An Introduction to the Theology of the Church of England in an Exposition of The Thirty-nine Articles* (London: Longmans, Green, and Co, 1875); E. J. Bicknell, *A Theological Introduction to the Thirty-Nine Articles of the Church of England* (London: Longmans, Green and Co, 1935); Griffith Thomas, *The Principles of Theology*, O. O'Donovan, *On The 39 Articles: A Conversation with Tudor Christianity* (Carlisle: Paternoster, 1986).

[384] E. A. Litton, *Introduction to Dogmatic Theology on the Basis of the Thirty-Nine Articles* (Houston, Texas: Classical Anglican Press, 2000) who has a section on limited atonement (pages 229-232) and is not sympathetic to the classic definition of it, does not even mention Article 31 there. The only commentary I can find in which the extent of redemption is actually discussed under Article 31 is J. Ellis, *A Defence of the Thirty-nine Articles of the Church of England* (London, 1700), 70 and this clearly takes the Calvinist view.

establish an anti-Calvinist dogma.[385]

5.3. *The Subscription Controversy (1771-1772)*

The expulsion of the Evangelical Calvinist undergraduates from Oxford in 1768 fuelled a national debate not just about student subscription to the Thirty-nine Articles but clerical subscription too. A group of clergy led by Theophilus Lindsey,[386] an Anglican minister with Arian and Socinian beliefs, met at the Feathers Tavern in the Strand in the summer of 1771. Their aim was to petition Parliament to abolish clerical subscription to the Articles. There was a fundamental resistance to the idea from many churchmen, with some even fearing it could lead to religious civil war and bloodshed.[387] A minority may have been inclined to tolerate more Unitarian influences but, says Gibson, "the initiatives occurred at a time when Methodism had made churchmen suspicious of schism and determined to defend orthodoxy."[388] This controversy produced two more contributions from Toplady's Reformed Evangelical Anglican pen.

Toplady's first response to the attempted liberalisation of subscription was his *Free Thoughts on the Projected Application to Parliament for the Abolition of Ecclesiastical Subscriptions* in November 1771. He set himself to defend what the British monarch's coronation oath calls "the true profession of the gospel, and Protestant reformed religion established by law."[389] In an age without "black, bigoted, unprotestant intolerancy" it was perfectly possible for these Unitarians to practice their religion freely and unmolested, so why could they not leave the established church alone? He accused them of sacrificing "conscience to profit, principle to ambition, and integrity to promotion,"[390] and of

---

385 T. R. Jones, *An Exposition of the Thirty-Nine Articles by the Reformers* (London: Hamilton, Adams and Co, 1849) which contains extracts from Cranmer, Latimer, Hooper, Ridley, Jewel and others on each of the Articles, shows (under Article 31 on pages 199-206) that their emphasis was firmly on the *sufficiency* (not the intent or extent) of the atonement, as against the Roman Catholic doctrine of the Mass which made the cross alone seem insufficient.

386 Toplady visited Lindsey's religious service to hear the liturgy and preaching after the latter had seceded from the Church in 1774, and describes the experience in a letter in *Complete Works*, 856-857.

387 See W. Gibson, *The Church of England 1688-1832: Unity and Accord* (London: Routledge, 2001), 98-100.

388 Gibson, *The Church of England 1688-1832*, 208.

389 *Complete Works*, 300.

390 *Complete Works*, 301.

"reforming us out of the reformation," so as to make the Church of England "the common sewer of every heresy under Heaven."[391]

A more developed and theological defence of subscription came in a sermon preached to the clergy in Exeter in May 1772. The Feathers Tavern Petition was defeated in the House of Commons just before this in February 1772, but the issue remained high on the agenda for some time, until the Petition was presented and finally defeated in May 1774. In his sermon, *Clerical Subscription No Grievance or The Doctrines of the Church of England Proved to be the Doctrines of Christ*, Toplady attempted to show that the teaching of Jesus was the same as that of the Church of England on fifteen doctrinal points: the inspiration and infallibility of Scripture, the unity of the Godhead, the plurality of persons in the divine essence, election, the pre-temporal covenant of redemption between the Father, Son, and Spirit for our redemption, original sin, penal substitutionary atonement, justification by faith alone (including the imputation of both the passive and active righteousness of Christ), conversion/effectual call, sanctification and the indwelling of the Holy Spirit, the necessity of good works, the final perseverance of the saints, unlimited providence, the immortality of the soul (against some who were teaching psychopannychia or 'soul sleep'), and the final resurrection of the body and eternal glory.

It is clear from inspecting the spread of doctrines he examines here that Toplady was aiming at both Arminian and Arian-Socinian errors. Underlying all these was, he thought, a naïve or insincere appeal to 'the Bible alone' as ultimate authority, to the detriment of the historic understanding of the Church of England as a fellowship of confessing believers holding to a written confessional statement. "The intentional destroyers of our national Church profess a mighty veneration for the Scriptures," he said, and they are "perpetually crying out in the much-prostituted words of the celebrated Chillingworth, 'The Bible, the Bible is the religion of Protestants.' It is certain that the Bible ought to be the religion of all Protestants: but it is no less certain that there are some Protestants whose religion has no more concord with the Bible than Belial has with Christ."[392] He begins on this footing and returns to the same sentiment near the end of his sermon. His conclusion is that objections to subscription to the Articles and objections to subscription to the Bible

[391] *Complete Works*, 303-304.
[392] *Complete Works*, 341.

itself are based on the same kinds of arguments, and undermining one would soon lead to the abolition of the other. Moreover, "if Arian subscription to Trinitarian articles is palpably dishonest, then, by all the rules of argument in the world, Arminian subscription to articles that are Calvinistic must and can be no less criminal."[393]

Throughout this work, Toplady attempted to show from the Scriptures that the Articles are a faithful epitome of the Bible's doctrine, and particularly of Christ's own teaching.[394] The clear implication he wishes to be drawn is that an attempt to free oneself from the Articles was in fact to declare independence from Christ himself.

5.4. *The Zanchi Tract War (1769-1772)*

Throughout the mid-eighteenth century the British often found themselves at war. To the East, the British East India Company was fighting the Anglo-Mysore and Anglo-Maratha Wars, and to the West a disturbance known as the American Revolutionary War promised to have important repercussions for the future. Back at home, Toplady also found himself enmeshed at this time in combat with a dangerous and skilful opponent.

In November 1769, some months after the publication of *The Church of England Vindicated*, Toplady published a translation of a work on predestination by Jerome Zanchius (1516-1590) which he entitled *The Doctrine of Absolute Predestination Stated and Asserted*.[395] This had been influential in his own spiritual development while he was a student and he had translated the work of "that most learned and evangelical divine" in 1760.[396] After some prompting from John Gill and others he overcame

---

[393] *Complete Works*, 616.

[394] One reason perhaps why he focuses on Christ's teaching is that some were driving a wedge between the epistles and the Gospels, as he intimates elsewhere, *Complete Works*, 745 note z.

[395] G. Lawton, *Within the Rock of Ages: The Life and Work of Augustus Montague Toplady* (Cambridge: James Clarke and Co, 1983), 34 suggests that this was a section of Zanchi's, *De Religione Christiana Fides* but this is not the case. I have consulted two earlier translations of that work, one printed by John Legat in Cambridge in 1599 and the other translated by D. Ralph Winterton and published in London in 1659, and it is clearly not the original source for Toplady's work. J. N. Tylenda, "Girolamo Zanchi and John Calvin: A Study in Discipleship as Seen Through Their Correspondence," in *Calvin Theological Journal* 10 (1975), 101 suggests that it was "Toplady's synopsis of Zanchi's *On the Nature of God, or on the Divine Attributes*, whose fifth book deals with predestination."

[396] *Complete Works*, 664.

his diffidence and decided the time was now right to publish this translation. Zanchi's book leans heavily on Luther's reply to Erasmus on the bondage of the will, as well as on Augustine, and covers election, reprobation, particular redemption, and various objections to those doctrines, concluding with a section promoting promiscuous gospel preaching to all and public teaching on predestination for the saints. The ultimate reason for focusing on this doctrine, he said, was Evangelical: "so far as the gospel is maimed, or any branch of the evangelical system is suppressed and passed over in silence, so far the gospel is not preached... scarce any other distinguishing doctrine of the gospel can be preached in its purity and consistency without this of predestination."[397]

In December 1769 John Wesley wrote to his Methodist colleague Walter Sellon to whom he had already set the task of answering John Owen's work on particular redemption. He asked him with regard to another treatise he was working on, "And pray add a word or two to Mr. Toplady, not only with regard to Zanchius, but his slander on the Church of England... He does certainly believe himself to be the greatest genius in England." Two months later he wrote again saying, "I believe it will be the best way to bestow a distinct pamphlet on Mr. Toplady. Surely wisdom will die with him! I believe we can easily get his other tract, which it would be well to sift to the very foundation, in order to stop the mouth of that vain boaster."[398] Evidently Wesley felt threatened by the arrival of the much younger Toplady on the scene.

It was Wesley himself, however, who made the most public response to the translation of Zanchi. He put out an abridgement of Toplady's work with the same title and published under Toplady's own name.[399] Three observations ought to be made on this abridgement. First, it does capture something of the general flow of Zanchius' argument and retain a few of the choicest quotations; as revision notes for an exam on

---

[397] *Complete Works,* 704. See also John Edwards, *Veritas Redux* (London, 1707), vii, x. which says, "The Divine decrees, the impotency of man's free will, original sin, grace and conversion, the extent of Christ's redemption, and perseverance are interwoven with the greatest and most substantial articles of the Christian faith... There is a necessity of preaching these in order to understand the main principles of our Christian belief."

[398] *The Works of John Wesley,* 13:44-45. In the edition of Wesley's letters edited by John Telford, *The Letters of John Wesley: Volume 5* (London, 1931), 167 this letter also contains Wesley's description of Toplady as a "lively coxcomb" (a conceited, showy person).

[399] "The Doctrine of Absolute Predestination Stated and Asserted by the Reverend Mr. A___ T___," in *The Works of John Wesley,* 14:190-198.

Zanchius' philosophy this material might have some use. Second, however, it removes entirely the biblical aspect of Zanchi's presentation. For example, in Toplady's translation there are around 350 quotations and citations from Scripture, around which the whole argument is built. In Wesley's abridgement there is just one biblical allusion ("Esau have I hated")[400] and that without giving the reference. This leaves an entirely different taste in the mouth and castrates the persuasive potential of the work for Christian readers. Finally, and most alarmingly, Wesley himself added a whole paragraph to the work, which was all his own work and seemed calculated to paint both predestination and Augustus Toplady in as bad a light as possible:

> The sum of all is this: One in twenty (suppose) of mankind are elected; nineteen in twenty are reprobated. The elect shall be saved, do what they will: The reprobate shall be damned, do what they can. Reader, believe this, or be damned. Witness my hand, A___ T___.[401]

Naturally, Toplady felt somewhat aggrieved by this gross misrepresentation. He replied to Wesley in *A Letter to the Rev. Mr. Wesley; Relative to his Pretended Abridgement of Zanchius on Predestination* pointing out that "In almost any other case, a similar forgery would transmit the criminal to Virginia or Maryland, if not to Tyburn." There were harsh laws at the time against forgery, which did indeed lead to the execution at Tyburn of one of Mr. Wesley's acquaintances in 1777.[402] Toplady thought it better to refute Wesley's falsehoods than take him to court for his plagiaristic libel. As far as this infamous final paragraph was concerned, for example, the numbers were wrong and certainly not Toplady's. In his opinion, "The kingdom of glory will both be more largely and more variously peopled than bigots of all denominations are either able to think, or willing to allow."[403] The summary of what he had written was also scurrilous, with entirely false implications. The elect are not saved "do what they will" but "chosen as

---

[400] *The Works of John Wesley*, 14:191.

[401] *The Works of John Wesley*, 14:198.

[402] See P. Fitzgerald, *A Famous Forgery: Being the Story of 'the Unfortunate' Doctor Dodd* (London: Chapman and Hall, 1865). For Wesley's letters to Dodd see *The Works of John* Wesley, 11:448-456.

[403] *Complete Works*, 726.

much to holiness as to heaven."[404]

Equally importantly, Toplady neither claimed nor thought that it was impossible for non-Calvinists to escape damnation.[405] That, of course, would have been a strange thing for him to assert, given that he was an Arminian himself for several years after his conversion and does not subsequently re-date his conversion to the year he became a Calvinist. He thought many Arminians were "pious, moderate, respectable men," adding, "Of these I myself know more than a few: and have the happiness to enjoy as much of their esteem, as they deservedly possess of mine."[406] He is careful not to say Arminians or even heretics such as Arius or Socinus are definitely excluded from heaven (God alone knows their destiny), though he is clear that if in heaven they are no longer Arminians, Arians, or Socinians there, but now stand corrected.[407] He can even be very positive about some other prominent Arminians such as Hammond, Bull, Tillotson, Sharp, and Stillingfleet, calling them eminent and worthy, "great ornaments to our church," and not to be mentioned without honour, even while he disagrees fervently with their Arminianism.[408]

Thus Toplady continued a family tradition of being at odds with Wesley, since two of his uncles had also argued personally and in print with the Methodist leader.[409] His reply to Wesley's cavalier attitude towards publishing is barbed and acerbic at times, which may be understandable perhaps and often even amusing, but not always a good example of the sort of approach to opponents recommended by the

---

[404] *Complete Works,* 735. See John Edwards, *Veritas Redux,* xxviii where this same "do what they will" accusation is called a senseless, vulgar suggestion and a trite and obsolete cavil which "should be despised by men of understanding."

[405] J. C. Ryle, *Christian Leaders,* 380 seems uncritically to buy Wesley's misrepresentation when he claims that Toplady "appears to think it impossible that an Arminian can be saved." Ironically, given Ryle's rather superior censure of Toplady, this completely overlooks all his positive statements about Arminians.

[406] *Complete Works,* 730. See also 732, "Whom do I condemn? Whom do I impiously consign to future punishment? I condemn no man. I dare not pronounce concerning any man's eternal state. Herein I judge not even Mr. Wesley himself." See also 761 (a prayer for Wesley who he trusts is not lost) and 840-844 (theological banter and evident mutual amusement in the conversation between Toplady and one of his staunch Arminian opponents, over a glass of wine, which ends on a positive and friendly note).

[407] *Complete Works,* 389.

[408] *Complete Works,* 614-615. See also 275 where he says that some great and good men are not Calvinists.

[409] See Lawton, *Within the Rock of Ages,* 7-8.

Apostle Paul in 2 Timothy 2:22-26.[410] Wesley may not have deserved better but that doesn't entirely excuse Toplady for, as it were, giving him both barrels in return. Wright claims that "the bitterness of his attack has scarcely a parallel in religious history,"[411] but this is a huge overstatement and reveals more of Wright's ignorance of Calvin and Luther (and Wesley!) in their polemics, than it does about Toplady.[412]

A certain sharpness against opponents cannot always be evil. See, for example, the inspired examples in Galatians 5:12 or Matthew 23. Perhaps, as J. C. Ryle rightly says, "different standards of taste" prevailed in former centuries. The mid eighteenth century is often summarised as one of *Sturm und Drang* (storm and stress), where biting passions and extreme emotions were uncorked in the arts: Goethe's classic Romantic tragedy, *The Sorrows of Young Werther* was published in 1774, and the painter William Hogarth (1697-1764) was vigorously satirical and often vicious in his moralising portrayals of English society. Toplady may appear tame by such contemporary standards. As Paul Helm has also more recently argued, "It has to be said that in [our] culture hamstrung by political correctness, Toplady's quaintly worded, fierce invective is amusing and refreshing. He made it clear that he was not being malicious, but (as he put it), 'It is not necessary to be timid in order to be meek.'"[413]

If some of Toplady's statements against Wesley do seem unworthy and unnecessarily harsh, when challenged about his tone he defended it as necessary: "Nor do I in the least repent of the manner in which I treated him. To have refuted the forgeries and perversions of such an assailant tenderly, and with meekness falsely so called, would have been like shooting at a highwayman with a pop-gun, or like repelling the sword of an assassin with a straw."[414] However, after Wesley responded

---

[410] Though this text was certainly one he dwelt on in his controversies and did attempt to obey: see his quotation of it in *Complete Works*, 34.

[411] T. Wright, *The Life of Augustus M. Toplady*, 88.

[412] Ella, *Augustus Montague Toplady*, 34 says that in comparison with Calvin's invective against Pighius, "Toplady treated Wesley with the manners and decorum of a gentleman and the analytical objectivity of a scientist." See my comments on Luther against Erasmus in "The Manifesto of the Reformation: Luther vs. Erasmus on Free Will," *Churchman* 123/3 (2009), 207-209.

[413] P. Helm, "Calvin, A.M. Toplady and the Bebbington Thesis," in M. A. G. Haykin and K. J. Stewart (eds.), *The Emergence of Evangelicalism: Exploring Historical Continuities* (Nottingham: Apollos, 2008), 216 citing *Complete Works*, 46, 48.

[414] *Complete Works*, 324.

again with a tract called *The Consequence Proved* in 1771, Toplady sat on his draft reply to this (called *More Work for Mr. Wesley*) for some weeks, and tried to remove "whatever might savour of undue asperity and intemperate warmth." If he failed to remove all traces of these, he confessed, "it is owing to the necessity I was under of exposing Mr. Wesley's unmanly and dishonest methods of attack."[415] Wesley did not even attempt to defend some aspects of his conduct or forgery, such as the claim that Toplady taught nineteen out of twenty people were going to hell or that all who disagreed with him were damned, presumably because they were indefensible. Equally indefensible, however, was his new counter-attack: in *The Consequence Proved*, Wesley compares the Calvinist God to a man who has his enemy's nine year old daughter raped so he can then strangle her to death because she has been 'deflowered.'[416]

Toplady rightly thought this impious (to say the least) and complained against "a man who is so liberally lamentable in his outcries against the doctrine of predestination, and carries to such horrid length his invectives against the purposes and providence of God."[417] It is no surprise that some Evangelicals refused to allow Wesley to use their churches.[418] Toplady's attempts at persuasion won him no friends amongst the Arminians, but he continued to pray for them and hope for them. He wrote to Ryland in 1773 that "The envy, malice, and fury of Wesley's party are inconceivable. But, violently as they hate me, I dare not, I cannot, hate them in return. I have not so learned Christ. — They have my prayers and my best wishes for their present and eternal salvation. But their errors have my opposition also."[419] Toplady's reputation has perhaps been unfairly maligned because the extravagant Arminian eccentricities of the great and famous John Wesley have been hushed up or too easily excused. It certainly does seem out of place for a man ordained nearly 50 years to behave the way Wesley did towards a fellow-Evangelical less than half his age. As Packer rightly says, Wesley's misrepresentations of Calvinism "argue a degree of prejudice and closed-

---

415 *Complete Works*, 730.

416 *The Works of John Wesley*, 10:373.

417 *Complete Works*, 761, 756.

418 A. Brown-Lawson, *John Wesley and the Anglican Evangelicals of the Eighteenth Century: A Study in Cooperation and Separation with Special Reference to the Calvinistic Controversies* (Durham: Pentland Press, 1994), 322.

419 *Complete Works*, 840. See the similar prayerful sentiment on 839 and at the start of the *Historic Proof* on 46.

mindedness which is almost pathological."[420]

So, even if his pen was sometimes mischievous, Toplady's heart was always to guard the gospel of God's mercy from those he saw as undermining it. After the Zanchius translation was published on the other side of the Atlantic, he wrote to a friend in New York about Wesley in 1773 saying, "I believe him to be the most rancorous hater of the gospel-system that ever appeared in this island. I except not Pelagius himself." As a young man in his twenties he had held back from publishing his translation of Zanchi for nine long years, fearful of offending Wesley and those on his side. But now, aged 32, he told his American correspondent, "I can never sufficiently bless God for giving me to see the day when I can truly affirm that I care not whom I displease when the inestimable truths of the gospel are at stake."[421] Thus we see it was not an irrational obsession with defeating Wesley which motivated Toplady. Indeed, he seems for many years to have been guilty of an unwarranted deference to the older man's fame and influence. If in later years this may have threatened to become an unhealthy fixation on demonstrating Wesley's perfidious errors, we can also see with crystal clarity that what truly motivated Toplady was proclaiming and defending the glorious gospel of God's mercy and grace. It was even his duty, he thought to pray for Wesley, writing, "O, that He, in whose hand the hearts of all men are, may make even this opposer of grace a monument of almighty power to save! God is witness how earnestly I wish it may consist with the divine will to touch the heart and open the eyes of that unhappy man."[422]

5.5. *The Historic Proof of the Doctrinal Calvinism of the Church of England (1774)*

It has been boldly said of the literature of this Arminian-Calvinist controversy that, "considered as permanent contributions to theological literature, the writings on either side are worthless."[423] This depends very much, however, on one's opinion of what is worthwhile. Toplady's great goal in writing his *Historic Proof* was to settle what is the true nature of

[420] J. I. Packer, "Arminianisms," in *Honouring the People of God: Collected Shorter Works of J. I. Packer Volume 4* (Carlisle: Paternoster, 1999), 300.

[421] *Complete Works*, 847. See also 722 where he says Wesley's theology is at odds with "evangelical truth."

[422] Quoted in Brown-Lawson, *John Wesley*, 328.

[423] Abbey and Overton, *The English Church in the Eighteenth Century*, 365.

the Church of England's 'official' doctrine, and to expose the cuckoo-like tendencies of alternative theologies which seek to make their home and their livings within its nest. For its exhaustive execution of that design it is both a worthy and exceptionally worthwhile contribution to Anglican historical and doctrinal literature. Bishop J. C Ryle declared Toplady's case to be unanswered and unanswerable.[424]

It seems at first as if Toplady's thesis in this hefty two-volume work is simple: "Our pulpits may declare for free-will; but the desk, our prayers, and the whole of our standard writings as a Church, breathe only the doctrines of grace," he declares in his introduction.[425] He does not however seek to demonstrate this by way of a doctrinal exposition of the Anglican formularies, as he did in *The Church of England Vindicated from the Charge of Arminianism* and his *Caveat against Unsound Doctrines.* Instead, he attempts to prove historically that the Articles are best understood in their Calvinistic sense (which was disputed by the Arminians) because those who framed them, and were martyred for them, were Reformed Calvinists themselves, as were all the major defenders and leaders of the Church until the advent of Archbishop Laud. Thus he attempts to establish not merely the Calvinism of the Anglican Standards, which he takes as a given, but the Calvinism of the Church more generally, understood as the bishops, clergy and people not just the written formularies.[426]

A similar argument had been used before, but not developed as fully as Toplady was to do. So for example, exactly one hundred years before *The Historic Proof,* Dr. John Owen wrote of the Reformed doctrines of election and justification that they had, "been asserted and defended by the greatest and most learned prelates [of the Church of England] in the foregoing ages, such as Jewell, Whitgift, Abbot, Morton, Usher, Hall, Davenant, Prideaux, etc., with the most learned persons of its communion, as Reynolds, Whitaker, Hooker, Sutcliffe, etc., and others innumerable; — testified unto in the name of this church by the divines, sent by public authority to the synod of Dort; — taught by the principal practical divines of this nation; and maintained by the most learned of the

---

[424] Ryle, *Christian Leaders,* 380.

[425] *Complete Works,* 47.

[426] See *Complete Works,* 192 especially where this line of attack is explicit in both point 1 and footnote y.

dignified clergy at this day."[427]

Toplady's primary exemplar in his historical endeavour was most probably Archbishop James Ussher (1581-1656). Ussher was not only one of the first ever students at Toplady's *alma mater* Trinity College, Dublin but had also played a leading role in its early formation, particularly after he was appointed Vice Chancellor in 1615, the same year in which he was closely involved in drawing up the firmly Reformed Irish Articles. He was keen to counter flourishing Roman Catholic historiography in the country and to establish a Protestant national identity.

In one of his most important works, *A discourse of the religion anciently professed by the Irish and Brittish* (sic),[428] Ussher made an exhaustive and compelling case that the faith professed by the clergy and people of Ireland prior to the Papal corruptions of the twelfth century onwards was in essence the same as that held by the Reformed establishment of his day. Examining copious amounts of evidence to determine the views of the early Irish and British churches on the doctrinal points at issue between Rome and the Protestant world, he showed how they had access to the Bible in the vernacular and stressed (with Augustine) the primacy of grace and predestination, even holding to justification *sola fide* and rejecting purgatory, penance, and other modern Roman distinctives. Calvinism was not only not new, as far as Ussher was concerned, it had a long, *bona fide*, and honourable pre-history in these islands.[429]

Ussher also wrote at a time when Arminianism, identified with the Pelagian heresy that had poisoned the national church, was rife. Toplady would therefore have been drawn to Ussher's work and his approach on several levels.[430] Indeed he cites the "excellent" and "learned" Prelate many times in the *Historic Proof*, always with warm appreciation for his scholarship, piety, and historical accuracy, speaking at one point of, "Archbishop Usher, whose enquiries were never superficial, and

---

[427] *A Vindication of Some Passages in a Discourse Concerning Communion with God* (1674) in *The Works of John Owen*, 2:304. See also 7:133 and 13:551-552.

[428] Second edition published in London 1631.

[429] See particularly A. Ford, *James Ussher: Theology, History, and Politics in Early-Modern Ireland and England* (Oxford: Oxford University Press, 2007), 123-124, and 275-279 on the continuing potency of Ussher's approach for the Church of Ireland.

[430] See H. Trevor-Roper, *Catholics, Anglicans, and Puritans: 17th Century Essays* (London: Secker and Warburg, 1987), 123, 144-149 on Ussher's work in its polemical context.

whose conclusions are never precipitate."[431]

Toplady had previously said that, "Not the sermons and private writings even of our reformers themselves are to be taken for authentic tests of our established doctrines as a Church; but those stubborn things called Articles and Homilies, which have received the sanction of law and the stamp of public authority."[432] Yet because Sellon and others had claimed the Reformers for their own opinions, Toplady now seeks to show that their sermons and writings in fact only confirm the case he has already made. This in turn shows how strong the case is for a Calvinist reading of the Articles in their historical context. He also demonstrates that Calvin himself had a significant influence on the Elizabethan church and that the Reformation settlement was praised and admired by significant Reformed voices from abroad such as Bucer, Zanchius, Bullinger, and Beza. Hence it must, therefore, have been in accord with internationally recognised canons of Reformed orthodoxy at the time, and not easily susceptible to obviously anti-Reformed interpretations. As a historical thesis it is vital that *The Historic Proof* must interact with the biggest name in Arminian historiography, Peter Heylyn. Toplady certainly has in his sights Heylyn's alternative thesis that the Articles are based on Melanchthonian Lutheranism and not Calvinism,[433] and he enjoys using Heylyn's evidence against Heylyn's own conclusions.[434]

As he sets about his task of proving the historic Calvinism of the established church, Toplady is also able to trace the historic lineage of Arminian doctrines. He examines the status and advocates of doctrines such as free will, election based on foreknowledge of faith and works, universal redemption (i.e. unlimited atonement), and the real possibility of final apostasy for the truly regenerate (i.e non-perseverance of the saints) in the course of his narrative. So, for example, he adduces copious amounts of evidence to prove that the following bishops and clergy are

---

[431] *Complete Works,* 89.

[432] *Complete Works,* 625. See also 615.

[433] *Complete Works,* 266-270. This argument continued to be replayed into the nineteenth century between, for example, John Overton *The True Churchman Ascertained* (London, 1802) and George Pretyman with his *A Refutation of Calvinism* (London, 1823). Overton says all the Reformers were Calvinists. Pretyman's conclusion (590) is that the Church of England is neither Lutheran nor Calvinist nor Arminian. Naturally, Toplady would have been most unsympathetic to Pretyman's argument, though on a personal level he would surely have empathised when the latter manfully decided to change his surname (to Tomline).

[434] See *Complete Works,* 58.

among those who held to definite atonement, and not to the indefinite universal atonement scheme of the Arminians: Ridley,[435] Latimer,[436] Bucer,[437] Rowland Taylor,[438] Thomas Causton and Thomas Higbed,[439] John Careless,[440] John Bradford,[441] John Melvin,[442] Andrew Willet,[443] and the British Delegation to the Synod of Dort.[444]

Wesley claimed some of these for his own view,[445] and later scholars of the 'Luther vs. Calvin school' have also attempted to claim that "the private sentiments of our Reformers" were inimical to Calvinist doctrine.[446] Toplady shows, however, that though they may have differed in their precise formulations, these theologians and martyrs affirmed the intrinsic sufficiency of the cross for all alongside a more particular

---

435 *Complete Works*, 132.

436 *Complete Works*, 141-143. Contra N. Tyacke, "Anglican Attitudes: some recent writings on English religious history, from the Reformation to the Civil War," in *Aspects of English Protestantism c. 1530-1700* (Manchester: Manchester University Press, 2001), 182 it is not clear that Latimer was what would later be termed an Arminian. The passages cited in P. White, *Predestination, Policy and Polemic: Conflict and Consensus in the English Church from the Reformation to the Civil War* (Cambridge: Cambridge University Press, 1992), 41-44 do not prove this, although his language that one can be in the book of life and then go out of it because of sin, or be in Christ and then out of him again, is certainly ill-judged and confused. See G. Corrie (ed.), *Sermons and Remains of Hugh Latimer* Volume 2 (Cambridge: Parker Society, 1844-1845), 175. Such language does have some precedent in the Augustinian tradition, e.g. Lombard, *The Sentences. Book 3*, 130 (3.31.1.7).

437 *Complete Works*, 150-151.

438 *Complete Works*, 166.

439 *Complete Works*, 168.

440 See *Complete Works*, 174 for the account of his examination on this point before a Roman Catholic commissary.

441 *Complete Works*, 181.

442 *Complete Works*, 191 note u.

443 *Complete Works*, 221.

444 *Complete Works*, 245.

445 See *The Works of John Wesley*, 10:425 where he claims Ridley, Hooper, and Latimer are universal redemptionists.

446 R. Laurence, *An Attempt to Illustrate those Articles of the Church of England which the Calvinists Improperly Consider as Calvinistical* (Oxford, 1820), page v.

intentionality and actual efficacy for the elect.[447] That is, none considered the cross merely to put all people into a saveable state, as the Arminians did. Bishop Davenant and Archbishop Usher were claimed by Sellon to have died Arminians.[448] In reality they affirmed a species of hypothetical universalism which included a dual intention in the cross, conditional for all but absolute and infallible for the elect,[449] as some delegates of the Westminster Assembly also did.[450] This was far from being Arminian, even if it was not precisely the same way of framing the Reformed doctrine as employed by Beza, Perkins, or Owen. Toplady was absolutely correct therefore to include them on his side of the argument, particularly considering their other doctrinally Reformed commitments. Toplady also includes evidence showing that the Apostolic Fathers held to particular redemption,[451] along with the medieval theologian Gottschalk of Orbais,[452] while the Arminian doctrine of universal redemption was held by the

---

447 One modern critic, in a needlessly provocative aside, insists that limited atonement is ruled out by the Articles and that those who hold to it ought not to offer themselves for ordination in the Church of England. See http://www.reform.org.uk/pages/bb/backtofuture.php and hear http://sthelens.audiop.org.uk/search/talk/51480. How this can be squared with this fine clergyman's professed admiration and enthusiasm for Whitefield, Toplady, and the other Reformed Evangelicals of the eighteenth century must remain a mystery. It must also be questioned how the Ordinal itself is contrary to limited atonement, since it outlines the business of a minister as including, "to feed and provide for the Lord's family; to seek for Christ's sheep that are dispersed abroad, and for his children who are in the midst of this naughty world, that they may be saved through Christ for ever... For they are the sheep of Christ, which he bought with his death, and for whom he shed his blood." This seems entirely in accord with the Reformed understanding of John 10 and verses such as Acts 13:48.

448 *Complete Works*, 245 note f.

449 See Carleton, *The Collegiat Suffrage*, 47-48 for Davenant and J. Ussher, *The Judgement of the late Archbishop of Armagh and Primate of Ireland, 1. Of the extent of Christs death and satisfaction* (London, 1658), 4-5, 13-15.

450 See my "Shades of opinion within a generic Calvinism: The Particular Redemption Debate at the Westminster Assembly," *Reformed Theological Review* (forthcoming, 2010). Edmund Calamy opened the Westminster debate on this issue saying, "I am farre from universall Redemption in the Arminian sence, but that that I hould is in the sence of our devines in the sinod of Dort... [Christ] did pay a price for all, absolute [intention] for the elect, conditionall [intention] for the reprobate, in case they doe believe." C. B. Van Dixhoorn, *Reforming the Reformation: Theological Debate at the Westminster Assembly 1642-1652* (Ph.D. diss., University of Cambridge, 2004), Volume 6, 202-203.

451 *Complete Works*, 83-88 on Clement, Ignatius, Polycarp, and the Epistle of Barnabus. Toplady was not a great lover of Patristics, believing that although there were some excellent things in the writings of the fathers, "the golden grains are almost lost amidst an infinity of rubbish," *Complete Works*, 82.

452 *Complete Works*, 92.

Roman Catholic Church,[453] and by a sect called the Ranters.[454] The reader is left in no doubt as to what Toplady is getting at here!

Since it was Wesley, Sellon, and other Evangelical Arminians who had occasioned this work, Toplady also traces the pre-history of their distinctive teachings on original sin, perfectionism, and justification which became more significant in this third stage of the Calvinist-Arminian controversy. First, Wesley claimed to be a firm advocate for original sin, a doctrine particularly obnoxious and offensive to Enlightenment intellectuals with their enthusiasm for the powers of human reason.[455] Yet this can be deceptive since he did not consider mankind to be as 'dead in sin' as the Reformed did, due to his doctrine of prevenient grace. As a defender of the gospel of grace it might seem that Toplady would be in favour of something with a name like 'prevenient grace': it sounds as if it might mean God's grace must precede human action which the Devonshire Vicar would heartily endorse, and did in fact preach.[456] However, going beyond the name we discover that Wesley's concept of prevenient grace taught that no-one this side of the first Christmas was actually spiritually dead and unable to respond to God for salvation. It is not that sinners, totally depraved since the Fall, need God to awaken and enlighten them before they can respond to the offer of salvation; rather, for Wesley, *all* have been sufficiently enlightened and their wills sufficiently restored that they can all now respond if they choose to. Original sin, therefore, no longer functions to render us unable to respond to God. Most clearly, in a sermon on Philippians 2:12 called *On Working Out Our Own Salvation*, Wesley says,

> Yet this is no excuse for those who continue in sin, and lay the blame upon their Maker, by saying, "It is God only that must quicken us; for we cannot quicken our own souls." *For allowing that all the souls of men are dead in sin by nature, this excuses none, seeing there is no man that is in a state of mere nature*; there is no man, unless he has quenched the Spirit, that is wholly void of the grace of God. No man living is entirely destitute of what is vulgarly called natural conscience. But this is not natural: It is more properly termed preventing grace. Every man has a

[453] *Complete Works*, 72-73.
[454] *Complete Works*, 79.
[455] *The Works of John Wesley*, 6:54-65.
[456] He uses the phrase "preventing grace" in a sermon on Isaiah 55:12 in Ella, *Augustus Montague Toplady*, 398. See Article 10.

greater or less measure of this... Every one has, sooner or later, good desires... Everyone has some measure of that light, some faint glimmering ray, which, sooner or later, more or less, enlightens every man that cometh into the world... So that no man sins because he has not grace, but because he does not use the grace which he hath.[457]

This is much more than what, in Reformed theology, is often termed 'common grace.' In *Predestination Calmly Considered* Wesley says that "there is a measure of free-will supernaturally restored to every man, together with that supernatural light which 'enlightens every man that cometh into the world.'"[458] For Wesley, although the Fall was catastrophic, after the incarnation and death of Christ some of the free will lost by Adam is restored and universally applied to all human beings. This 'universal enablement' empowers people to respond to the gospel, or not, as they choose. Wesley's prevenient grace is therefore resistible grace; this concept is directly contrary to Calvinist conclusions about invincible grace as well as original sin and the bondage of the will. It was however much more in tune with the Enlightened spirit of the age.

Toplady would heartily agree with one modern theologian who concludes his study of Wesleyan biblical arguments for prevenient grace saying, "Prevenient grace is attractive because it solves so many problems, but it should be rejected because it cannot be exegetically vindicated."[459] Toplady links the doctrine of his opponents to the Jesuit doctrines of resistible grace and partial depravity, showing how these denials of Reformed doctrine are related.[460] Indeed, this Wesleyan form of prevenient grace has some strong associations with the theology of Luis Molina (1535-1600), a Spanish Jesuit famous for his theory of 'middle knowledge' which William Lane Craig summarises thus: "God desires and has given grace sufficient that all people should be saved. If some believe and others do not, it is not because some received prevenient

---

457 *The Works of John Wesley*, 6:512; emphasis added. See also 6:509.

458 *The Works of John Wesley*, 10:229-230. See also 10:392 and 7:189.

459 T. R. Schreiner, "Does Scripture Teach Prevenient Grace in the Wesleyan Sense?" in T. R. Schreiner and B. A. Ware (eds.), *Still Sovereign: Contemporary Perspectives on Election, Foreknowledge, and Grace* (Grand Rapids: Baker, 2000), 246. See C. H. Pinnock's confession that "the Bible has no developed doctrine of universal prevenient grace, however convenient it would be for us if it did," in "From Augustine to Arminius: A Pilgrimage in Theology," in C. H. Pinnock (ed.), *The Grace of God, the Will of Man: A Case for Arminianism* (Grand Rapids: Academie, 1989), 22.

460 *Complete Works*, 72.

grace and calling while others did not. Rather, the efficacy of God's grace in our lives is up to us, and every person, however unconducive his circumstances, is called and moved by God in a measure sufficient for salvation."[461]

Toplady links the Arminian doctrine of original sin to the Arminian doctrine of free will and predestination, spending time and effort to establish the Reformed teaching of the Reformers on these intimately related points so as to refute Wesley's novel scheme.[462] He also wrote a short essay on original sin in which he explored these connections more fully, citing Articles and Homilies as well as Scripture to full effect.[463] Wesley said in 1745 that he thought the truth of the gospel was "within a hair's breadth" of Calvinism, particularly in terms of this doctrine.[464] Yet on close inspection it is right to conclude that the differences are certainly not trivial and "though Wesleyanism and Calvinism come in this instance so close together, they are in reality worlds apart,"[465] as both sides increasingly recognised. The terminology might sound similar, but the concepts behind the words were very different indeed.

Second, on perfectionism, we noted earlier how this was one of the distinctive doctrines around which Wesley rallied his own following.[466] This was another doctrine in which Wesley appears to have given great redemptive-historical significance to the incarnation at the expense of continuity between the testaments. For Wesley, just as original sin had given way to prevenient grace for all when Christ had entered the world, so also it was now (since Christ) no longer true that everyone was a sinner. People may quote 1 Kings 8:46, 2 Chronicles 6:36 and Ecclesiastes 7:20 ("There is not a just man upon earth that doeth good, and sinneth not"), but Wesley's response to such texts was to say,

> Without doubt, thus it was in the days of Solomon. Yea, thus it was from Adam to Moses, from Moses to Solomon, and from Solomon to Christ. There was *then* no man that sinned not. Even

[461] W. L. Craig, "Middle Knowledge: A Calvinist-Arminian Rapprochement?" in Pinnock, *The Grace of God, the Will of Man*, 157-158.
[462] *Complete Works*, 136-137, 155, 182, 186-187.
[463] *Complete Works*, 409-416.
[464] See *The Works of John Wesley*, 8:284-285.
[465] W. R. Cannon, *The Theology of John Wesley: With Special Reference to the Doctrine of Justification* (New York: University Press of America, 1974), 102.
[466] See above, chapter 3.

from the day that sin entered into the world, there was not a just man upon earth that did good and sinned not, *until* the Son of God was manifested to take away our sins... It is of great importance to observe, and that more carefully than is commonly done, the wide difference there is between the Jewish and the Christian dispensation.[467]

Only proofs from the New Testament would, therefore, be of use in refuting Wesley's perfectionism which claimed that it was possible for a Christian to be free of sin and perfect in love, something which could happen instantaneously or slowly, at death or many years before. In Wesley's own words perfection is not infallibility or perfect physical health but, "loving God with all our heart, mind, soul, and strength. This implies, that no wrong temper, none contrary to love, remains in the soul; and that all the thoughts, words, and actions, are governed by pure love."[468] The command, "thou shalt love thy neighbour as thyself" was, for him, not just a command but a promise which could be fulfilled in this life.[469]

It was, of course, a gift for Toplady that Pelagius had also taught a form of Christian perfection, "[t]hat when converted, men might, and numbers of men did, live without sin; perfectly obeying the law."[470] This allowed him to link Wesley with the arch-heretic once more and establish a line of heterodox descent for the doctrine which had been linked in the past with free will, justification by works, conditional election and, Toplady ironically added, unholiness of life.[471] Again, speaking of a Ranter who had been deprived of his living in the Church in 1581, Toplady said this man denied predestination, was an avowed perfectionist, and that he was an uncharitable bigot, adding, "Who, on this occasion, can help thinking on Messieurs John Wesley and Walter Sellon?"[472] Examining sixteenth century Reformer Hugh Latimer's contrary teaching on the subject, Toplady concludes "it necessarily follows, that the supposition of possible perfection on earth, is the most fanatic dream, and the most

---

[467] *The Works of John Wesley*, 6:9-10; emphasis added.
[468] *The Works of John Wesley*, 11:394.
[469] *The Works of John Wesley*, 6:415. See also 6:413.
[470] C. Hodge, *Systematic Theology: Volume 3* (Peabody, MA: Hendrickson, 1999), 250 on Pelagianism.
[471] *Complete Works*, 52 note i.
[472] *Complete Works*, 79.

gigantic delusion, which can whirl the brain of a human being."[473] Elsewhere he said, "To hold this heresy is the very quintessence of delusion."[474] Yet this is the doctrine Wesley described as "the grand depositum" of the Methodists.[475] It is not often noted that Toplady's famous hymn which begins "Rock of ages, cleft for me," which appeared in the *Gospel Magazine* of 1776, is actually directed against this very teaching, its full title being *A Living and Dying Prayer for the Holiest Believer in the World.* Note particularly verse two, which has added resonance in this polemical context:

> Nothing in my hand I bring,
> Simply to thy cross I cling;
> Naked come to thee for dress,
> Helpless, look to thee for grace:
> Foul, I to the fountain fly,
> Wash me, Saviour, or I die.[476]

The most perfect believer in this life remained always naked, helpless, and foul. To sing otherwise would be to declare an independence from Christ and a spiritual self-sufficiency which no believer could ever attain.[477]

Finally, as well as the more obvious Calvinist-Arminian touchstones, Toplady pays especial attention in *The Historic Proof* to the doctrine of justification. Was this most Protestant and Evangelical shibboleth also an issue between Calvinists and Arminians in the 1770s? Indeed it was, thanks to the controversy surrounding Wesley's Methodist Conference in 1770. Wesley had been losing patience with the Evangelical

---

[473] *Complete Works*, 141. See also 197.

[474] *Complete Works*, 321.

[475] Schwenk, *Catholic Spirit*, 41.

[476] See Ella, *Augustus Montague Toplady*, 436.

[477] Wright, *The Life of Augustus M. Toplady*, 175 tells the story of how in 1775 when preaching at St. Botolph's, Aldersgate before the Mayor, Aldermen, and common council Toplady deliberately asked them to sing a dodgy hymn he found in the church's book, merely to then refute its perfectionist teaching: "It was certainly a curious object lesson to set a great congregation to sing a hymn with the sole purpose of impressing upon them the viciousness of its doctrines; and we may safely assume not only that the congregation were embarrassed, and that the hymn was sung with no great fervour, but that every individual among them remembered the incident (and thus accomplished Toplady's desire) until his dying day." How ironic that this was only a few yards from where Wesley's heart had been "strangely warmed" in 1738, in a church which now boasts a stained glass window to his memory!

Calvinists and was somewhat estranged from the Countess of Huntingdon at this time having written her a frank letter of stinging rebuke which she found deeply offensive.[478] He chose this moment to return to the Arminian distinctives, but particularly to justification and its relationship to holiness with which he had been wrestling. The Minutes of the Conference were "so drafted as to appear to teach, Roman-style, that a man's works are the ground of his acceptance with God."[479] For example, as well as rebuking the conference for leaning "too much towards Calvinism," Wesley told them that, "every believer, till he comes to glory, works for, as well as *from*, life... We have received it as a maxim that 'a man is to do nothing in order to justification.' Nothing can be more false... Is not this salvation by works? Not by the *merit* of works, but by works as a *condition*... we are every hour and every moment pleasing or displeasing to God, 'according to our works.'"[480]

This caused quite a furore, and the Countess immediately banned Wesley from ever preaching in her chapels, and seemed to regard his planned attendance at Trevecca College's anniversary celebrations as a sinister bid to influence the students.[481] Fletcher was forced to resign as president of Trevecca, the theological training college of the Evangelical movement, and Joseph Benson another Arminian lecturer there was dismissed. All the students were required to write a response to the Minutes, "with the threat that Lady Huntingdon would expel anyone 'who did not *absolutely* disavow and renounce' them."[482]

Even after a Calvinist delegation attended the next Methodist Conference and persuaded it to clarify its position in a more irenic direction, John Fletcher published six *Checks to Antinomianism* over the next few years (1771-1775) as a defence of the position taken in the controversial Minutes. Toplady, therefore, thought it vital to note what the Church of England's teaching was on justification. He notes for example a Jesuit argument that some of the Thirty-nine Articles were susceptible to a Catholic interpretation, including "justification not by faith alone," immediately censuring some churchmen for holding this despite the fact

---

[478] For the background to the relationship between Wesley and the Countess at this stage see F. Cook, *Selina Countess of Huntingdon: Her Pivotal Role in the 18th Century Evangelical Awakening* (Edinburgh: Banner of Truth, 2001), 271-277.

[479] J. I. Packer, "Arminianisms," 301.

[480] For the text of the Minutes see e.g. Cook, *Selina*, 278-279.

[481] See Cook, *Selina*, 280.

[482] A. Harding, *Selina, Countess of Huntingdon* (Peterborough: Epworth, 2007), 136.

that "The Thirty-nine Article (*sic*) themselves are neither patient nor ambitious of what the Jesuit called a Catholic sense."[483] He also attacks what he calls "Mr. Wesley's lax Protestantism," in relation to the doctrine of justification.[484] He often speaks of "free justification" to contrast it with either the Wesleyan or Roman Catholic scheme, which he sees as adding works to the gratuitous act of God.

To those who speak of a second justification by works at the last day, Toplady says (while expounding Latimer's writings) that "works... will not be the ground even of that public and declarative justification, which will be predicated of the elect at that awful season."[485] He addresses Arminian arguments that Bucer was of their opinion with regards to justification by works and the merit of human obedience,[486] speaks of the Roman Catholic denial of justification by faith alone being "a tenet, now, as common to Arminians, as ever it was to Papists,"[487] and digresses a little at one stage to establish that "If righteousness, either justification itself, or any part of the righteousness which justifies, come by the law, accrue, though ever so remotely, to any sinner, by or through his own conformity to the moral law; then it would follow that Christ is dead in vain."[488] One of his most powerful arguments is that the Reformation martyrs died for holding to Calvinist tenets, and against the accusation that these led to antinomianism Toplady cries out,

> If any man seriously supposes that Calvinism relaxes the sinews of evangelical or moral duty, let him consider the holiness, the honesty, and the heroism, of those Calvinist saints, whose sufferings and deaths redden the Protestant Calendar, and who resisted even unto blood, striving against sin.[489]

Wesley, however, had moved away from the Reformation emphases and so, as Clifford nicely puts it, "the doctrine of a standing church became a source of discord for a divided Protestantism."[490] Wesley's heart may have been strangely warmed in 1738 after a reading from Luther's commentary

---

483 *Complete Works*, 67.
484 *Complete Works*, 75 note u.
485 *Complete Works*, 139. See also 223 on first and second imputation.
486 *Complete Works*, 158.
487 *Complete Works*, 168.
488 *Complete Works*, 167.
489 *Complete Works*, 174.
490 A. C. Clifford, *Atonement and Justification: English Evangelical Theology 1640-1790. An Evaluation* (Oxford: Clarendon Press, 1990), 170.

on Romans, but he later rejected Luther's commentary on Galatians and its doctrine of justification, calling it a "dangerous treatise" and saying, "he is quite shallow in his remarks on many passages, and muddy and confused almost on all... often dangerously wrong... how blasphemously does he speak of good works and of the Law of God."[491]

To the later Calvinist emphasis that justification was not only bare acquittal but that Christ's righteousness was also imputed to the believer, Wesley was equally opposed, believing it to undermine all good works. He complained of those who said, "that Christ had done, as well as suffered, all; that his righteousness being imputed to us, we need none of our own; that seeing there was so much righteousness and holiness in Him, there needs none in us; that to think we have any, or to desire or seek any, is to renounce Christ; that from the beginning to the end of salvation, all is in Christ, nothing in man..." This was "a blow at the root... of all holiness, all true religion... For wherever this doctrine is cordially received, it leaves no place for holiness."[492] To believe this doctrine of double imputation is, therefore, to betray Christ as Judas did and 'to stab him in the house of his friends,' said Wesley.

Toplady, however, patiently demonstrated that the non-imputation of our sins as well as the imputation of Christ's righteousness (both his active obedience to clothe the sinner, as well as the blood of his so-called passive obedience) were equally a part of the testimony of the Church of England regarding this doctrine.[493] Indeed, with his 1771 hymn called *The Assurance of Faith* he ensured it would be celebrated for centuries to come:

> A debtor to mercy alone,
> Of covenant mercy I sing;
> Nor fear with thy righteousness on,
> My person and off'rings to bring:
> The terrors of law and of God
> With me can have nothing to do;
> My Saviour's obedience and blood
> Hide all my transgressions from view.[494]

---

[491] *The Works of John Wesley*, 1:315-316.

[492] *The Works of John Wesley*, 10:366.

[493] See e.g. *Complete Works*, 197 (on Galatians 3.12), 199, 310. See also *The Works of John Owen*, 5:164.

[494] See Ella, *Augustus Montague Toplady*, 429 for the hymn's dates of publication in the *Gospel Magazine*.

5.6. *Conclusion*

We have not touched on some of Toplady's other controversial writings in the last 3 years of his life, but they follow a similar pattern to those we have examined here. He sought in every one to defend the gospel of salvation by God's mercy alone from its detractors. Being in such debt to that mercy himself, he felt a deep obligation to protect it for others. At the conclusion of *The Historic Proof*, Toplady asks a question which is still able to raise a wry smile or disappointed sigh from many members of the established church: "Is there a single heresy, that ever annoyed the Christian world, which has not its present partisans among those who profess conformity to the Church of England?" The reason why Arians, Socinians, and others had been able to take hold was that they "all made their way through that breach at which Arminianism entered before them," he said.[495] The Church had been softened up for more advanced liberalism by the insincere subscription and compromised theology of Arminian churchmen.

All Toplady's polemics with Wesley and other Arminians were therefore motivated by this desire to guard "the true profession of the gospel" within the pale of the establishment. To his mind, the gospel of grace was best protected by preaching and proactively preserving the so-called doctrines of grace. He was Reformed because he was Evangelical. Hence he called for clergy to stand firm and "steadfastly abide by the doctrines of the reformation, which are found to quadrate [square] so exactly with the glorious gospel of the blessed God."[496] For Toplady, Reformed theology was simply the most biblical and thought-through way of keeping works out of the equation of salvation and giving all the glory to God. The great question for him was "who shall stand entitled to the praise and glory of a sinner's salvation?"[497] Should we sing the praise of covenant mercy alone, or add another object of praise (our free will, or our works) to the church's hymns and spiritual songs?

Throughout this body of work, there is no sense of Toplady trying to impose a philosophical grid onto the Bible or of a slavish attachment to any one particular theologian whose system he feels duty bound to propagate. He criticises others who twist Scripture and detach verses from

---

[495] *Complete Works*, 275-276.

[496] *Complete Works*, 351-352.

[497] *Complete Works*, 353.

their contexts in order to fit their preconceived doctrinal notions.[498] He knew this was a temptation. His "system" was the gospel itself, and here we might contrast Toplady's attachment to *The Gospel Magazine* with Wesley's organ of propaganda, entitled *The Arminian Magazine*, which had the explicit aim that, as Wesley put it, "the bulk of the Magazine (as the very title implies) should treat of universal redemption."[499]

It should also be noted that although we have spent our time examining his doctrinal and controversial works, Toplady was much more than the arch-enemy of Arminians. Nor was the tone of polemical engagement his only idiom. His hymns and poems indicate he was a man of deep sensitivity and profound reflection, while his *Works* contain sermons and essays on themes as diverse as the chronology of English history, the millennium, cruelty to animals, the natural history of birds and meteors, and female education. Yet at a time when James Watt was tinkering with his ground-breaking steam engines which would power Britain's industrial revolution, Augustus Toplady was convinced that the Church of England already possessed the greatest possible source of spiritual motivation and power in the Reformed, Evangelical, and Protestant faith — and this was his greatest joy and obsession.

A few months shy of his thirty-eighth birthday, as Augustus Montague Toplady's short life drew to a close and he was literally on his death bed, news came to him of rumours suggesting he had renounced his faith. He wished, it was being said, to repent, in the presence of Mr. Wesley, of all he had said and done in these controversies. In what must have been a dramatic scene, and against the doctor's orders, he dragged himself out of bed and into his pulpit so as to correct those rumours (sometimes said to have been spread by Wesley himself) and reaffirm his faith. In his "dying avowal" he said, "I pray God to give the 'perfect' liars grace and repentance to the acknowledgement of the truth. And may every blessing, of the upper, and of the nether springs, be the portion of those who maintain, who experience, and adorn, the glorious gospel of the grace of God!"[500]

Wesley himself did indeed spread malicious rumours about Toplady's manner of death once he was buried, saying that he died in black despair, uttering horrendous blasphemies. Toplady's friends

---

498 E.g. *Complete Works*, 639. See also 643.

499 *The Works of John Wesley* 14:364.

500 *Complete Works*, 34; inverted commas around 'perfect' added.

received gloating letters commiserating them on the fact that their friend had been "a dud squib." Sir Richard Hill demanded Wesley produce his authority for such slanderous and nefarious tales, adding the testimony of thirteen friends who had been with Toplady when he died. No reply ever came, and all Wesley would say to two of Toplady's friends who sought him out for a response was, "Those that are for peace will let those things alone."[501] Wesley, it seems, could get away with almost anything against those that differed from him and hush it up, not with private apology or repentance, but with an appeal to Evangelical unity and peace.

It would be wrong, however, to leave the last word to Wesley. Toplady himself must be permitted to summarise all that we have seen in this examination of his writings. Some of his very last recorded words to a friend were these:

> My dear friend, those great and glorious truths which the Lord, in rich mercy, has given me to believe, and which he has enabled me (though very feebly) to stand forth in defence of, are not (as those, who believe not or oppose them, say) dry doctrines, or mere speculative points. No. But, being brought into practical and heart-felt experience, they are the very joy and support of my soul; and the consolations, flowing from them, carry me far above the things of time and sense.[502]

Thus in the year that Captain Cook aboard HMS *Resolution* discovered the sun-kissed beaches of the Hawaiian Islands, Augustus Montage Toplady reached the shores of a true and eternal Paradise, having lost none of his resolve.

---

[501] For the whole sordid tale see Ella, *Augustus Montague Toplady*, 331-340. See also Wesley's winking regurgitation of the slander in 1784 in *The Works of John Wesley*, 4:278.

[502] *Complete Works*, 36.

6. Rehabilitating Toplady And Reviving Reformed theology

Whilst the Calvinistic doctrines were the language of our pulpits as well as of our Articles, the Reformation made a swift and extensive progress. But ever since our Articles and our pulpits have been at variance, the Reformation has been at a stand.

- Augustus Toplady (1769)

6.1. "Those that are for peace will let those things alone"?

In November 1787, nearly a decade after Toplady died, a young Charles Simeon, destined to be the leader of the Evangelicals into the next century, met with the aging John Wesley. The conversation (though it is not recounted in Wesley's journal) has often been cited as evidence that Calvinists and Arminians are in essence agreed on fundamentals:

Simeon: Sir, I understand that you are called an Arminian; and I have been sometimes called a Calvinist; and therefore I suppose we are to draw daggers. But before I consent to begin the combat, with your permission I will ask you a few questions, not from impertinent curiosity, but for real instruction. Pray, Sir, do you feel yourself a depraved creature, so depraved, that you would never have thought of turning unto God, if God had not first put it into your heart?

Wesley: Yes, I do indeed.

Simeon: And do you utterly despair of recommending yourself to God by any thing you can do; and look for salvation solely through the blood and righteousness of Christ?

Wesley: Yes, solely through Christ.

Simeon: But, Sir, supposing you were first saved by Christ, are you not somehow or other to save yourself afterwards by your own works?

Wesley: No, I must be saved by Christ from first to last.

Simeon: Allowing then that you were first turned by the grace of God, are you not in some way or other to keep yourself by your own power?

Wesley: No.

Simeon: What then, are you to be upheld every hour and every moment by God, as much as an infant in its mother's arms?

Wesley: Yes; altogether.

Simeon: And is all your hope in the grace and mercy of God to preserve you unto his heavenly kingdom?

Wesley: Yes; I have no hope, but in him.

Simeon: Then, Sir, with your leave, I will put up my dagger again; for this is all my Calvinism; this is my election, my justification by faith, my final perseverance: it is, in substance, all that I hold, and as I hold it: and therefore, if you please, instead of searching out terms and phrases to be a ground of contention between us, we will cordially unite in those things wherein we agree.[503]

We ought to notice that Simeon begins (if this account is accurate and does actually relate to Simeon himself)[504] not by claiming to *be* a Calvinist but by saying he has "sometimes" been called one. Normally, he did not want to identify either with Calvinists or Arminians, claiming to be "no friend to systematizers in Theology..." He had "no doubt that there is a system in the Holy Scriptures; (for truth cannot be inconsistent with itself)," but he was "persuaded that neither Calvinists nor Arminians are in exclusive possession of that system."[505] Wesley, on the other hand, although he does not recount the conversation, identified Simeon on both occasions when the two met as very much like his own designated successor as leader of the Arminians, J. Fletcher of Madeley — "two kindred souls," he called them in 1784;[506] Simeon "breathes the very spirit

---

[503] The conversation is recounted in C. Simeon, *Helps to Composition, or Six Hundred Skeletons of Sermons* 1st American ed. (Philadelphia, 1810), Volume 1, xviii note o, and Carus, *Memoir of the Rev. Charles Simeon* (London, 1847), 105-106.

[504] The dialogue is prefaced, "A circumstance within the Author's knowledge reflects so much light upon this subject, that he trusts he shall be pardoned for relating it. A young minister, about three or four years after he was ordained, had an opportunity of conversing familiarly with the great and venerable leader of the Arminians in this kingdom; and, wishing to improve the occasion to the uttermost, he addressed him nearly in the following words..." It seems likely that it does refer to Simeon himself, but a small doubt remains due to the third person references.

[505] C. Simeon *Horae Homileticae or Discourses (in the Form of Skeletons) upon the Whole Scriptures* (London, 1819), Volume 1, 4-5.

[506] T. Jackson (ed.), *The Works of John Wesley* (Grand Rapids: Baker, 2007), 4:294.

of Mr. Fletcher," he repeated in his journal in 1787.[507] That is not to say that Simeon was an Arminian, of course (I don't believe he was), only that his Calvinism was either unseen or sufficiently confused as to not attract the attention of the man who had been Calvinism's self-proclaimed nemesis for fifty years and had made such harsh pronouncements against it.

Perhaps Simeon was somewhat naïve in his youthful enthusiasm to sidestep decades of serious discussion and be considered (like a consummate ecclesiastical politician) sympathetic to both sides. Yet the debate was not, as many may wish it to be, one merely of timing and where to place the emphasis — as if Calvinists like Whitefield held to divine sovereignty but did not appeal for human decisions, or that they simply ignored parts of Scripture that did not at first blush seem to fit their preconceived system, or that they were abstract theologisers who needed Arminians to teach them how to speak to real people. To say Arminian doctrines of free will could be used alongside Calvinist teaching concerning divine providence and grace as if they were not necessarily contradictory perhaps sounded irenic.[508] Yet what are we to make of Simeon's comment that, "It is supposed by many, that the doctrines of grace are incompatible with the doctrine of man's free-will; and that therefore the one or the other must be false. But why so?" — or his assertion that, "it is possible, that the truth, may lie, not exclusively in either, nor yet in a confused mixture of both, but in the proper and seasonable application of them both."[509] It seems likely that Simeon's misunderstanding that the two systems could be pastorally blended to obtain a supposedly better, more biblical, balance played straight into synergistic Arminian hands, and I suspect the more experienced Wesley was well aware of this. Toplady would have said something like, "evangelical truth knows nothing of this harlequin assemblage."[510]

Second, it ought to be pointed out that Simeon, narrating events two decades previously, does most of the talking in this famous exchange,

---

[507] *The Works of John Wesley*, 4:403. Since Simeon was ordained deacon in 1782 and priest in 1783 the conversation (if between Simeon and Wesley) took place between 1785-1787 (3-4 years after he was ordained, as he says), and hence the November 1787 meeting is the most likely occasion contra e.g. H. Moule, *Charles Simeon: Pastor of a Generation* (Fearn, Ross-shire: Christian Focus, 1997 [1892]), 83 who dates it to 1784.

[508] See Simeon, *Helps to Composition*, xxi.

[509] Simeon, *Helps to Composition*, xvi.

[510] A. M. Toplady, *The Complete Works of Augustus Toplady* (Harrisburg, Virginia: Sprinkle Publications, 1987), 722.

putting words into the older man's mouth. Hence we learn more here about Simeon than we do about Wesley himself. Very skilfully, he skirts round some of the actual areas of contention to present himself in a very positive light to a generation of Evangelicals weary of internecine warfare. For example, he asks whether Wesley "feels himself depraved" not whether he *is* or *was* totally depraved before his conversion which, because of his doctrine of prevenient grace or 'universal enablement,' he would not have been able to answer in the affirmative like a Calvinist.

As he re-sheaths his dagger Simeon declares, "this is all my Calvinism; this is my election." We should note, however, that he has at no point actually addressed the doctrine of election in the conversation. Presumably this is because he knew full well that Wesley believed in predestination on the basis of foreseen faith and perseverance, and not on the basis of God's gratuitous unmerited choice alone. This was no small point but goes to the very heart of the predestination debate, though in his noble and heroic crusade for Evangelical unity Simeon evidently feels it is merely "searching out terms and phrases to be a ground of contention." Admittedly, by the late eighteenth century some may have gone too far into an unhealthy hyper-Calvinism or into arguing about words in an unwholesome way. Yet there was real gospel-minded concern at the heart of people's anxiety about Wesley, which is not apparent from the way Simeon deals with him here.

Third, it is hardly right to acquit Wesley (and Arminianism) of synergistic views of salvation simply on the basis of his own protestations and denials. Which Christian theologian ever admitted openly to teaching salvation by works? Yet that is not to say every Christian theologian avoids that trap or tendency as a clear implication of their system. Calvinists and Arminians alike need to guard themselves from inconsistency with their own profession and the dangers on either side of them.

Nevertheless, Simeon's view of Wesley and of Arminianism has become the dominant note in Evangelicalism. Differences between Calvinists and Arminians are too often evaded and fudged for the sake of unity and peace so that someone who dredges them up is considered factious and unnecessarily combative — "a cynic, a bear, a Toplady," as Wesley put it in his usual sour way.[511] It is remarkable how often individuals have covered a drift towards Arminianism "with professions of indifference to theological aridities," as one writer so strikingly puts

---

[511] *The Works of John Wesley*, 10:414.

it.[512] In such an atmosphere is it possible or even desirable to rehabilitate Toplady the controversialist? Or is it better to leave his polemical work in obscurity and remember him only for a handful of classic hymns?

In my view, it is imperative that Toplady is heard again in proper context by both Evangelicals and Anglicans. It is vital, as Paul Helm rightly notes, to see clearly that the Evangelical participants in the eighteenth century controversy, "certainly did not think that what united them was greater than what divided them. The occurrence of the Calvinist-Arminian division was very serious, fairly permanent, and sad."[513] Toplady for one would not have considered himself an Evangelical first and Reformed second if that meant his supposed unity with Wesley was more important than their disagreements. He may acknowledge some common ground, but resisted the idea that the issues at stake between them on predestination, the atonement, perfectionism, original sin, and justification were of only secondary importance, to be placed on one side for the sake of a common witness. In his view, the Reformed Evangelical Anglican testimony to God's saving grace in the gospel must remain entirely unadulterated, or eventually be swallowed up. We forget this at our peril.

6.2. *'Catholic Spirit' and Contending for the Mainstream*

Toplady took the stance he did because he was aware of the longer term historical perspective. Garry Williams expounds this elegantly in the context of the debate over the origins of 'Evangelicalism':

> If we think that evangelicalism began in the 1730s, then Wesley and [Jonathan] Edwards become its most important fathers. This means that evangelicalism was from its origin equally divided between Reformed and Arminian theology. Neither could claim to be the mainstream doctrinal position. In this sense it is easy to see how Bebbington's analysis serves to give a strong foothold to Arminianism within the evangelical movement by making foundational one of its most noted proponents. If, however, we reconsider the origins of evangelicalism and find that it is a

[512] A. Cromartie, 'Hale, Sir Mathew (1609–1676),' *Oxford Dictionary of National Biography* (Oxford: Oxford University Press, 2004).

[513] P. Helm, "Calvin, A.M. Toplady and the Bebbington Thesis," in M. A. G. Haykin and K. J. Stewart (eds.), *The Emergence of Evangelicalism: Exploring Historical Continuities* (Nottingham: Apollos, 2008), 215.

Reformational and Puritan phenomenon, then the picture looks very different.

> The magisterial Reformers on the Continent and in England during the sixteenth century and the Puritans of the seventeenth were almost without exception committed to a Reformed account of the doctrine of election. Evangelicalism then becomes aboriginally Reformed on the doctrine of election rather than divided. The position taken by John Wesley on election becomes a deviation along with that of Philip Melanchthon and his Lutheran followers, and Jacobus Arminius and the Remonstrants. With such a historical perspective, Reformed theology becomes the authentic evangelical mainstream of three centuries, and the historical case for the foundational status of Arminianism is undermined.[514]

We have argued this very thesis above, just as Toplady himself did, to demonstrate that Reformed theology is indeed not only the Evangelical mainstream of three centuries but also the Anglican mainstream. It is therefore an essential ingredient in any account of Evangelical or Anglican identity, though its foundational role is too often unappreciated or not given sufficient prominence by those more concerned with the current political exigencies of balancing competing factions within the constituency.[515] It can also be effectively sidelined by those who see Anglican identity as defined essentially by the Caroline divines after the Restoration, when the Reformed puritans were removed from the Church. As Patrick Collinson so helpfully writes, "That our modern conception of Anglicanism commonly excludes Puritanism is both a distortion of a part of our religious history and a memorial to one of its

---

[514] G. J. Williams, "Enlightenment Epistemology and Eighteenth-Century Evangelical Doctrines of Assurance," in Haykin and Stewart (eds.), *The Emergence of Evangelicalism*, 374.

[515] For example, in an otherwise very helpful book, Richard Turnbull, *Anglican and Evangelical?* (London: Continuum, 2007) acknowledges (13-14) the formative role of the Reformation on Anglicanism and the association of the Church of England with the Reformed tradition (45) but he does not wish to make "a simple claim that the Anglican heritage is Reformed or Evangelical" (47). He goes along with the Bebbington thesis that Evangelicalism began in the 1730s (51) and hence disagreements over Arminian points (like the "esoteric debate" about the extent of the atonement, 57) are foundational to Evangelicalism (66, posing an unhelpfully false dichotomy between the extent of the atonement and the extent of the offer of salvation).

more regrettable episodes."[516] Just as Peter Heylyn's revisionist account of Anglican history was the perfect weapon to justify harsh treatment of those ejected Calvinists,[517] so also if the common story told of Anglicanism today makes such people seem marginal to the history they could easily again be sidelined, persecuted, or ejected.

What Evangelicalism *is* has changed, of course, and this can be explained by noting the different influences upon those calling themselves Evangelical. As Richard Turnbull rightly says, "Evangelicalism is a spectrum."[518] Anglicanism has also changed, due to the transformative influence of other movements and traditions which have intruded upon the Reformed foundations of the established church in the last two hundred years. What I have tried to show is how Toplady defended the idea that Anglicanism and Evangelicalism *were* Reformed. Indeed, how they could trace their roots back many centuries to anti-Pelagianism within the mainstream church and not just to the traditional radical succession of Wycliffe, the Lollards, and Hus. This descriptive task is undertaken in imitation of Toplady's own conviction that what once *was* Anglican and Evangelical now ought to be considered authentically so again. To be Reformed in either movement is not to be an interloper or gatecrasher but to assert a rightful claim to the doctrinal heritage. This claim needs pressing more firmly, more often.

Naturally there were and are disagreements amongst the Reformed worldwide on issues such as infant baptism and infant salvation, infralapsarianism, Reformed versions of hypothetical universalism, the imputation of the active obedience of Christ, eternal justification, and so on. Some positions in these controversies have a greater claim to be mainstream Reformed than others. Yet what Anthony Milton says of Dort holds true of the Reformed constituency more generally, "For all the sometimes acerbic exchanges, occasional disagreements and resentments, all of the delegates — the British divines included — were bound together by a common conviction that what

---

[516] P. Collinson, *The Elizabethan Puritan Movement* (Oxford: Clarendon Press, 1967), 467. See the similar conclusion of S. Hampton, *Anti-Arminians: The Anglican Reformed Tradition from Charles II to George I* (Oxford: Oxford University Press, 2008), 273.

[517] A. Milton, *Laudian and Royalist Polemic in Seventeenth-Century England: The Career and Writings of Peter Heylyn* (Manchester: Manchester University Press, 2007), 214.

[518] Turnbull, *Anglican and Evangelical?*, 89.

united them was more important than what divided them."[519]

Therefore, recapturing the Reformed teaching which alone can truly re-animate Anglicanism holds the key not just to the stability of worldwide Anglicanism but also to renewed efforts at evangelistic ecumenism. Not, it should be noted, the ecumenism whereby Anglican theologians try as hard as they can to sound like Roman Catholics or to appreciate the spirituality of the East; but a domestic reunification of conformist and nonconformist in passionate mission together to win the nation for Christ, as well as a renewed sense of fellowship across international borders with those who love the doctrines of grace, whatever their ecclesiological commitments. Most Reformed Evangelical Anglicans feel instinctively that they have more in common with Reformed brethren elsewhere than they do with other Anglicans of a different stripe. The greatest American influences on Evangelicals in the Church of England, for example, are not from The Episcopal Church (still officially part of the same Anglican Communion) but names like John Piper, Mark Driscoll, Mark Dever, Tim Keller, and Don Carson from Reformed Baptist and Presbyterian traditions.

As an explicitly Reformed church, the Church of England was able to play a leading role, as we have seen, as part of an international Reformed community in the sixteenth and seventeenth centuries. This did not continue long and as MacCulloch says, "Anglicanism in later centuries has continued steadily to distance itself from international Protestantism."[520] The growth of empire eventually brought England its own peculiar brand of isolationist internationalism — what is now the Anglican Communion — through which Churchmen could play at global ecclesiastical politics and connexionalism without having to deal much with Presbyterians and Anabaptists. Yet in the eighteenth century Whitefield, Toplady, and others were keen and able to foster good relations with gospel-hearted men and women outside the pale of the Establishment in a way that Arminians like Wesley simply were not. Indeed, Wesley's well-known aversion to dissenters (what Toplady calls

[519] A. Milton (ed.), *The British Delegation and the Synod of Dort (1618-1619)* Church of England Record Society Volume 13 (Woodbridge, Suffolk: The Boydell Press, 2005), lv.
[520] D. MacCulloch, *Reformation: Europe's House Divided 1490-1700* (London: Penguin, 2004), 510.

his "illiberal and malevolent spleen against the Protestant dissenters"),[521] isolated him from this larger constituency. His father in fact "wrote so furiously against the Dissenters that he was actually imprisoned for it,"[522] and it seems John Wesley particularly reviled Baptists.[523] All this left him open to accusations of lack of cooperation and catholicity, and of building a personal empire.

On the Calvinistic side of the revival, however, cross-denominational mission was not uncommon. Whitefield endeared himself to Baptists and Presbyterians alike at home and abroad with his commitment to Reformed orthodoxy, which they were not used to hearing from Anglican clerics. Toplady was not the last Evangelical to lament that many who were at heart Anglicans felt they had to attend free churches instead to hear their own Church's Reformed doctrine, because the preaching was so poor and unsound at their parish church.[524] This remains an issue today,[525] but it also reveals that there is much common ground to be explored between Anglican and non-Anglican Reformed constituencies which could prove fruitful in the future if they can continue to work together. In this way Reformed theology could be a revivifying force not just for the established church but also for the cause of the gospel more widely as it strengthens the bonds of fellowship across denominational lines.

Care must always be exercised with ecumenical and international commitments, however. They may lead in unforeseen and unwanted directions. A 'catholic spirit' (greatly praised in the eighteenth century),[526]

---

[521] *Complete Works,* 723. Wesley particularly disliked nonconformists for their Predestinarian doctrine, their manner, tone, language and length of prayers, and their style of singing. Toplady contrasts this with Wesley's fondness for Roman Catholicism. In his open letter to Wesley in *The Journals of George Whitefield* (Edinburgh: Banner of Truth, 1960), 583 Whitefield rebuked Wesley for claiming that "no Baptist or Presbyterian writer... knew any thing of the liberties of Christ."

[522] I. H. Murray, *Heroes* (Edinburgh: Banner of Truth, 2009), 49.

[523] M. Haykin, "'The Sum of All Good': John Ryland, Jr. and the Doctrine of the Holy Spirit," *Churchman* 103/4 (1989), 333.

[524] *Complete Works,* 661.

[525] Anecdotally, I was told recently by a senior free church minister that if a Reformed Evangelical was appointed to the Anglican church in his town then he would lose at least half his congregation to it.

[526] See Murray, *Heroes,* 47-83 on Whitefield's catholicity; *The Works of John Wesley,* 5:492-504 for a sermon called "Catholic Spirit;" and of course J. L. Schwenk, *Catholic Spirit: Wesley, Whitefield, and the Quest for Evangelical Unity in Eighteenth-Century British Methodism* (Plymouth: Scarecrow Press, 2008).

can be an excellent expression of gospel-motivated humility, but should not compromise a prior fundamental commitment to Reformed theology. Alliances for limited co-belligerence are one thing; expressions of full communion and fellowship with those who deny the basic tenets of Reformed (and therefore truly Anglican and Evangelical) theology, however, would give away something extraordinarily precious. That could turn out to be a step in the direction of the doctrinally latitudinarian (or as it is called today, 'generously orthodox') stance of Gilbert Burnet and John Wesley, who thought Arminianism should be tolerated for the sake of evangelistic goals and to strengthen the Church against Unitarian influences. History demonstrates that a liberalising tide is not easily turned back and as David Wells has recently stated concerning Evangelicalism, "it is now rather clear that the toleration of diversity slowly became an indifference toward much of the fabric of belief that makes up the Christian faith."[527] Moreover, Anglicanism and Evangelicalism are not simply anti-Liberal coalitions, and to attempt to redefine them as such (rather than in more positive, doctrinally Reformed ways) would be a somewhat naïve method of giving the ball away to the historic opponents of the unconditional love and grace of God.

6.3. *Reassessing Wesley's 'Open' Evangelicalism*

One of the problems with rehabilitating Toplady is the effect it can have on perceptions of Wesley. Was the great Methodist hero of the revival really as bad as Toplady (and many others among his contemporaries) painted him? Did he really say and do the things we have documented here, and if so should we really be rummaging around in such filth and grime instead of focusing on the positive? So, writes Iain Murray, "If Wesley's theology was confused, why some might ask, should we value his memory today? The answer is that it is not in his theology that his real legacy lies. Christian leaders are raised up for different purposes. The eighteenth century Evangelicals were primarily men of action, and in that role, John Wesley did and said much which was to the lasting benefit of many thousands."[528]

It is true that Wesley had vision, determination, and fantastic organisational ability. He was a gifted leader and a prolific author with an

---

[527] D. Wells, *The Courage to be Protestant: Truth-lovers, Marketers and Emergents in the Postmodern World* (Nottingham: IVP, 2008), 8

[528] I. H. Murray, *Wesley and Men Who Followed* (Edinburgh: Banner of Truth, 2003), 79.

eye for propagating his brand of Christianity in flexible and skilful ways. He loved Jesus, wanted others to know and love him too, and strove to be more holy. However, problems always arise when we start to identify and equate too closely what our particular movement within Christendom is doing with what God is doing. When that happens, anyone who desires to challenge the movement's teaching or behaviour can come to be regarded as criticising God himself. This is how it feels for some when they hear criticism of the charismatic, powerful, and successful Evangelical John Wesley. "Look at what he did for God!" they say, "And how people were converted and lives changed." Yet we must not be afraid of a 'warts and all' look at our heroes and great ones. God is gracious and uses all kinds of people, but even Conservative Evangelical churches are not immune from becoming cults, idolising our leaders and papering over their serious faults which God and history see all too well.

William Ames, who attended the Synod of Dort and was an advisor to its President, wrote that the Arminians' doctrine, "as it is taken by the mass of their supporters, is not strictly a heresy, that is, a major lapse from the gospel, but a dangerous error tending toward heresy. As maintained by some of them, however, it is the Pelagian heresy."[529] Packer's apposite comment on this is that, "Ames' words alert us to the fact that Arminianisms vary, so blanket judgments are not in order: each version of post-Reformation semi-Pelagianism must be judged on its own merits."[530] Wesley's variety of this theological error was serious but not entirely fatal, since he was thankfully inconsistent in its application as we have noted. His polemics and ways of operating against opponents, however, rightly earned him some firm rebukes and should continue to horrify Christians of sincerity who love the truth today. We may need to be more sparing in our use of the label "heresy" and (recalling Wesley's portrayal of the Calvinist God as a child-molester and worse than the devil) in the ways we paint our opponents.

It may be difficult to model amicable disagreement in our churches where Congregationalist Arminian Credobaptist Anglicans sometimes coexist alongside Reformed Paedobaptists with Presbyterian leanings. It takes patience and a costly investment in personal relationships that we don't always feel we have time for in the busyness of

---

[529] W. Ames, *De Conscientia* IV:iv q.4 as quoted in "Arminianisms," in *Honouring the People of God: Collected Shorter Writings of J. I. Packer Volume 4* (Carlisle: Paternoster, 1999), 303.

[530] Packer, "Arminianisms," 303.

our programmes. Tearing strips off each other is always easier, as is demonising our opponents and forgetting to exercise charitable judgment.[531] We may know we're right on the theology and on the Thirty-nine Articles. Yet 1 Corinthians 8 reminds us that if we think we "know" then we do not yet know as we ought. Love, grace, and gentle persuasion are needed to win those who we perceive to be opposing the gospel of grace. Wesley himself said, "Cannot a man hold *distinguishing grace*, as it is called, but he must distinguish himself for passion, sourness, bitterness?"[532] He didn't always take his own medicine, as we've seen, but he does remind us that cranky Calvinists are often their own worst enemies. If we are cold, competitive, and driven while being relative strangers to "the inner relaxation and gaiety witnessed to by such outstanding workers for God as Paul, George Whitefield, and C. H. Spurgeon, who knew themselves to be carried along and kept every moment by divine power,"[533] then it is because we are not sufficiently Reformed in practice and therefore no great advert for our liberating and gracious theology. Much true repentance here would do us immeasurable good.

Wesley once said that he and his followers were "Church-of-England men. They love her Articles, her Homilies, her Liturgy, her discipline, and unwillingly vary from it in any instance."[534] Yet when he came to compile the Articles for use in his new denomination, Article 17 on predestination was — of course! — conspicuous by its absence in Wesley's amended list (along with other things he formerly confessed to love). Where the Reformers had said, "the godly consideration of predestination, and our election in Christ, is full of sweet, pleasant, and unspeakable comfort," Wesley wished to deny the saints this comfort in his revised Articles, because he disliked the implications of such teaching.

Toplady claimed Wesley had "erected himself into the leader of a sect." He drew particular attention to Wesley's use of a foreign bishop with dubious credentials to preside at irregular ordinations of Wesley's preachers who then dressed and officiated as if clergy of the Church of England. These ordinations, Wesley claimed, were valid but irregular, and

---

[531] See Mike Ovey's comments on demonising others and exercising charity in M. Downes, *Risking the Truth: Handling Error in the Church* (Fearn, Ross-shire: Christian Focus, 2009), 178-179.

[532] *The Works of John Wesley*, 10:414; emphasis original.

[533] Packer, "Arminianisms," 304.

[534] *The Works of John Wesley*, 8:350.

Toplady suggests that Wesley wanted the Greek prelate who performed these ordinations also to consecrate him as a "bishop at large," so he could multiply such ordinations on his own.[535] Toplady said, "I abhor every thing that even looks like persecution, for principles merely religious,"[536] which is a very good thing for Wesley since Toplady found it exceedingly difficult to understand why someone of his views did not simply avail themselves of the generous provisions of the Act of Toleration and leave the Church of England.

More than once, Toplady and other Evangelicals suggested that the motives of those who disagreed with Reformed Anglican teaching but who continued to draw a stipend from the Church may be less than pure. The status and financial rewards of establishment credentials were evidently an adequate compensation for cauterising one's conscience it seems: "Let them retract their subscriptions, not by word and in tongue only, but in deed and in truth, by renouncing the preferments, as well as the doctrines, of the church; and all the world will call them honest men."[537] Evangelicals today may say similar things with some cogency to liberals in their denominations who, like the eighteenth century establishment, tolerate immorality but abhor institutional "irregularities" (such as crossing parish boundaries). As Owen put it in the seventeenth century, "Had a poor Puritan offended against half so many canons as they opposed articles, he had forfeited his livelihood, if not endangered his life... divers prelates were so zealous for the discipline and so negligent of the doctrine of the church."[538]

It should be remembered, however, that subscription to doctrinal articles is actually a matter of good order, of which liberals in power often claim to be the upholders. Such casuistry, like that which claims to be

---

[535] *Complete Works*, 719, 727.

[536] *Complete Works*, 205.

[537] *Complete Works*, 302. See also 311 where he accuses such people of "subscribing to articles they do not believe, merely for the sake of temporal profit or aggrandisement." It was common amongst the Evangelicals in this period to point to the hypocrisy of those who did not actually believe the formularies they subscribed to. We have already noted Whitefield and Wesley doing this but see also William Romaine's blistering Preface to his *A Practical Comment on the Hundred and Seventh Psalm* (London, 1767) which is a model example of this approach, citing not only Articles, Homilies, and Liturgy in support of Reformed Evangelical convictions, but the writings of late seventeenth century bishops such as Reynolds and Beveridge as well.

[538] *A Display of Arminianism* in W. H. Goold (ed.), *The Works of John Owen* (Edinburgh: Johnstone and Hunter, 1850-1853), 10:9.

able with integrity to teach one thing while believing another, should be exposed. There has never been a golden age where all truly subscribed *ex animo* and were entirely free of hypocrisy, of course. We ought to be realistic about human nature. Yet that is no excuse to abandon the idea of a public standard of doctrine, and discipline, in our church life.

However, let it not be forgotten that Toplady the Evangelical originally said this sort of thing to Wesley the Evangelical. He accused him (basically) of entryism, an attempt to become part of an organisation simply in order to subvert it. When Evangelical Anglicans claim, therefore, to have the title deeds to Anglicanism, Toplady, Whitefield, Romaine and others remind us that those deeds are made out to *Reformed* Evangelical Anglicans and not to lowest-common-denominator Evangelicalism, and even less to 'open' or Arminian flavours. These may have less right to be counted authentically Anglican than devotees of other brands of churchmanship often attacked as cuckoos in the nest. We must take care that we are not double-minded ourselves. It is foolish, after all, to attempt to point the finger at others for their hypocrisy if our own fingers are crossed behind our backs when we pledge to uphold certain doctrines and practices in our churches and in our families.

6.4. *Taking Toplady Home*

Toplady made his point about the doctrinal Calvinism of the Church of England painstakingly, repeatedly, and with devastating logical effectiveness. It would be naïve, however, to assume that just because someone has done masses of research and written the big knock-down book with an irrefutable argument that this will immediately transform the academy or the church. Life is rarely so simple. In the same way, just as the church in Jeremiah's day was not safe simply because they trusted in "the temple of the Lord, the temple of the Lord, the temple of the Lord" (Jeremiah 7:4), neither will twenty-first century Anglicans reform their churches simply by chanting, "The Articles of Religion, the Book of Common Prayer, the Homilies and Canons!" That would be romantic antiquarianism. Such formularies must be believed and obeyed (as they point us to Christ) not just tenaciously held onto like prize exhibits in a museum.

There is great power in the gospel. It is the power of God for the salvation of everyone who believes (Romans 1:16). It also has the potential, through the conversion of individuals who put it into practice in every area of their lives, to transform whole communities and nations. This was demonstrated in the afterglow of the eighteenth century revivals through men like William Wilberforce, and is acknowledged even by secular historians. Harvard scholar Nancy Cott, for example, in her history of marriage and sexuality, mentions as an aside the power in Christians' hands to affect their society: "since transgressive forms of sexuality have been allowed into the open," she says, "they will not be tucked back behind the curtains — not without a nationwide religious revival."[539] Mere politics cannot correct the huge changes we have witnessed in this area over the last few decades. It is not just our politicians who have let us down by publicly abandoning Christian moral standards. Have we prayed fervently and worked ceaselessly for the revival of the gospel which alone can truly bring change to our nation? A little secular marginalisation may do us some spiritual good, if it forces us back onto our knees before God.

British monarchs have, since the *Coronation Oath Act* of 1689, promised to maintain "the true profession of the gospel, and Protestant Reformed religion established by law." In changed times, the question asked of Queen Elizabeth II in 1953 may not be put to the next monarch. Yet it remains a question of vital relevance for all in the Church of England. So let us not simply ask, "Will he?" but "Will we?" Surrounded by the great cloud of witnesses from the Anglican and Evangelical Reformed tradition, "Will *you* to the utmost of your power maintain the Laws of God and the true profession of the Gospel? Will *you* to the utmost of your power maintain in the United Kingdom the Protestant Reformed Religion?"

Yet ultimately it is not to monarchs or even to faithful clergy that we must look. God alone is able to breathe new life into the establishment, as local churches plough on with the work of evangelism, the pursuit of holiness, and prayerfully bold engagement in the wider structures of the denomination. If God was at work in Broad Hembury, Haworth, Huddersfield, Yelling, Truro, and Weston Favell (to name just a few of the centres of eighteenth century Evangelical awakening) then we need not look solely to Brompton or Bishopsgate, Langham Place or Lambeth Palace to lead us or give us hope. The smallest chapels and parishes become strategic in God's eyes when the doctrines of grace return to their pulpits and streets, and he is at work there. As Whitefield once said, "nothing makes a town so worthy of a gracious soul's remark of esteem, as its having many of God's dear children for its inhabitants.

[539] N. F. Cott, *Public Vows: A History of Marriage and the Nation* (London: Harvard University Press, 2002), 215.

Bethany, though a little place, is more famous because it was the town of Martha and Mary, than if Alexander had fought in it one of his greatest battles."[540]

We do not yet know the names of the villages and towns which may be hallowed by future generations as the settings for great works of God's Spirit in our century. What we do know is that it is only as the spiritual lamps go on in places like Barnsley, Tranmere, Oswestry, St. Neots, Balham, and Fowey that the people of England will again 'walk in the light' and tuck the unhappy immorality and greed of the current day back behind the curtains. So to take Toplady's message home, let's heed his urgent summons to action:

> Blessed be God, the doctrines of grace are again beginning to lift up their heads amongst us; a sign, it is to be hoped, that the Holy Spirit hath not quite forsaken us, and that our redemption from the prevailing errors of the day draweth near. Now, if ever, is the time for all who love our Church and nation in sincerity to lend a helping hand to the ark, and contribute, though ever so little, to its return.[541]

---

540 L. Gatiss (ed.), *The Sermons of George Whitefield: Part 2* (Watford: Church Society, 2010), 129.

541 *Complete Works,* 665.

For further reading

D. W. Bebbington, *Evangelicalism in Modern Britain: A history from the 1730s to the 1980s* (London: Routledge, 1989)

A. Dallimore, *George Whitefield: The Life and Times of the Great Evangelist of the 18th Century Revival* 2 volumes (Edinburgh: Banner of Truth, 1970, 1980)

G. M. Ella, *Augustus Montague Toplady: A Debtor to Mercy Alone* (Eggleston, Durham: Go Publications, 2000)

S. Hampton, *Anti-Arminians: The Anglican Reformed Tradition from Charles II to George I* (Oxford: Oxford University Press, 2008)

M. A. G. Haykin and K. J. Stewart (eds.), *The Emergence of Evangelicalism: Exploring Historical Continuities* (Nottingham: Apollos, 2008)

M. A. Noll, *The Rise of Evangelicalism: The Age of Edwards, Whitefield and the Wesleys* (Leicester: Apollos, 2004)

J. C. Ryle, *Christian Leaders of the Eighteenth Century* (Edinburgh: Banner of Truth, 1978 [1885])

A. M. Toplady, *The Complete Works of Augustus Toplady* (Harrisonburg, Virginia: Sprinkle Publications, 1987)

N. Tyacke, *Aspects of English Protestantism c. 1530-1700* (Manchester: Manchester University Press, 2001)

L. Gatiss (ed.), *The Sermons of George Whitefield* 2 volumes (Watford: Church Society, 2010)

Latimer Publications

LS 01	*The Evangelical Anglican Identity Problem – Jim Packer*	*LS 17*	*Christianity and Judaism: New Understanding, New Relationship – James Atkinson*
LS 02	*The ASB Rite A Communion: A Way Forward – Roger Beckwith*	*LS 18*	*Sacraments and Ministry in Ecumenical Perspective – Gerald Bray*
LS 03	*The Doctrine of Justification in the Church of England – Robin Leaver*	*LS 19*	*The Functions of a National Church – Max Warren*
LS 04	*Justification Today: The Roman Catholic and Anglican Debate – R. G. England*	*LS 20/21*	*The Thirty–Nine Articles: Their Place and Use Today – Jim Packer, Roger Beckwith*
LS 05/06	*Homosexuals in the Christian Fellowship – David Atkinson*	*LS 22*	*How We Got Our Prayer Book – T. W. Drury, Roger Beckwith*
LS 07	*Nationhood: A Christian Perspective – O. R. Johnston*	*LS 23/24*	*Creation or Evolution: a False Antithesis? – Mike Poole, Gordon Wenham*
LS 08	*Evangelical Anglican Identity: Problems and Prospects – Tom Wright*	*LS 25*	*Christianity and the Craft – Gerard Moate*
LS 09	*Confessing the Faith in the Church of England Today – Roger Beckwith*	*LS 26*	*ARCIC II and Justification – Alister McGrath*
LS 10	*A Kind of Noah's Ark? The Anglican Commitment to Comprehensiveness – Jim Packer*	*LS 27*	*The Challenge of the Housechurches – Tony Higton, Gilbert Kirby*
LS 11	*Sickness and Healing in the Church – Donald Allister*	*LS 28*	*Communion for Children? The Current Debate – A. A. Langdon*
LS 12	*Rome and Reformation Today: How Luther Speaks to the New Situation – James Atkinson*	*LS 29/30*	*Theological Politics – Nigel Biggar*
LS 13	*Music as Preaching: Bach, Passions and Music in Worship – Robin Leaver*	*LS 31*	*Eucharistic Consecration in the First Four Centuries and its Implications for Liturgical Reform – Nigel Scotland*
LS 14	*Jesus Through Other Eyes: Christology in a Multi-faith Context – Christopher Lamb*	*LS 32*	*A Christian Theological Language – Gerald Bray*
LS 15	*Church and State Under God – James Atkinson*	*LS 33*	*Mission in Unity: The Bible and Missionary Structures – Duncan McMann*
LS 16	*Language and Liturgy – Gerald Bray, Steve Wilcockson, Robin Leaver*	*LS 34*	*Stewards of Creation: Environmentalism in the Light of Biblical Teaching – Lawrence Osborn*
		LS 35/36	*Mission and Evangelism in Recent Thinking: 1974–1986 – Robert Bashford*
		LS 37	*Future Patterns of Episcopacy: Reflections in Retirement – Stuart Blanch*

LS 38	*Christian Character: Jeremy Taylor and Christian Ethics Today – David Scott*
LS 39	*Islam: Towards a Christian Assessment – Hugh Goddard*
LS 40	*Liberal Catholicism: Charles Gore and the Question of Authority – G. F. Grimes*
LS 41/42	*The Christian Message in a Multi-faith Society – Colin Chapman*
LS 43	*The Way of Holiness 1: Principles – D. A. Ousley*
LS 44/45	*The Lambeth Articles – V. C. Miller*
LS 46	*The Way of Holiness 2: Issues – D. A. Ousley*
LS 47	*Building Multi–Racial Churches – John Root*
LS 48	*Episcopal Oversight: A Case for Reform – David Holloway*
LS 49	*Euthanasia: A Christian Evaluation – Henk Jochemsen*
LS 50/51	*The Rough Places Plain: AEA 1995*
LS 52	*A Critique of Spirituality – John Pearce*
LS 53/54	*The Toronto Blessing – Martyn Percy*
LS 55	*The Theology of Rowan Williams – Garry Williams*
LS 56/57	*Reforming Forwards? The Process of Reception and the Consecration of Women as Bishops – Peter Toon*
LS 58	*The Oath of Canonical Obedience – Gerald Bray*
LS 59	*The Parish System: The Same Yesterday, Today And For Ever? – Mark Burkill*
LS 60	*'I Absolve You': Private Confession and the Church of England – Andrew Atherstone*
LS 61	*The Water and the Wine: A Contribution to the Debate on Children and Holy Communion – Roger Beckwith, Andrew Daunton–Fear*
LS 62	*Must God Punish Sin? – Ben Cooper*
LS 63	*Too Big For Words?: The Transcendence of God and Finite Human Speech – Mark D. Thompson*
LS 64	*A Step Too Far: An Evangelical Critique of Christian Mysticism – Marian Raikes*
LS 65	*The New Testament and Slavery: Approaches and Implications – Mark Meynell*
LS 66	*The Tragedy of 1662: The Ejection and Persecution of the Puritans – Lee Gatiss*
LS 67	*Heresy, Schism & Apostasy – Gerald Bray*
LS 68	*Paul in 3D: Preaching Paul as Pastor, Story–teller and Sage – Ben Cooper*
LS69	*Christianity and the Tolerance of Liberalism: J.Gresham Machen and the Presbyterian Controversy of 1922 – 1937 – Lee Gatiss*
LS70	*An Anglican Evangelical Identity Crisis: The Churchman – Anvil Affair of 1981–1984 – Andrew Atherstone*
LS71	*Empty and Evil: The worship of other faiths in 1 Corinthians 8-10 and today – Rohintan Mody*
LS72	*To Plough or to Preach: Mission Strategies in New Zealand during the 1820s – Malcolm Falloon*
LS73	*Plastic People: How Queer Theory is Changing Us – Peter Sanlon*

Latimer Publications

LB01	*The Church of England: What it is, and what it stands for – R. T. Beckwith*
LB02	*Praying with Understanding: Explanations of Words and Passages in the Book of Common Prayer – R. T. Beckwith*
LB03	*The Failure of the Church of England? The Church, the Nation and the Anglican Communion – A. Pollard*
LB04	*Towards a Heritage Renewed – H.R.M. Craig*
LB05	*Christ's Gospel to the Nations: The Heart & Mind of Evangelicalism Past, Present & Future – Peter Jensen*
LB06	*Passion for the Gospel: Hugh Latimer (1485–1555) Then and Now. A commemorative lecture to mark the 450th anniversary of his martyrdom in Oxford – A. McGrath*
LB07	*Truth and Unity in Christian Fellowship – Michael Nazir-Ali*
LB08	*Unworthy Ministers: Donatism and Discipline Today – Mark Burkill*
GGC	*God, Gays and the Church: Human Sexuality and Experience in Christian Thinking – eds. Lisa Nolland, Chris Sugden, Sarah Finch*
WTL	*The Way, the Truth and the Life: Theological Resources for a Pilgrimage to a Global Anglican Future – eds. Vinay Samuel, Chris Sugden, Sarah Finch*
AEID	*Anglican Evangelical Identity – Yesterday and Today – J.I. Packer and N.T. Wright*
IB	*The Anglican Evangelical Doctrine of Infant Baptism – John Stott and J.Alec Motyer*
BF	*Being Faithful: The Shape of Historic Anglicanism Today – Theological Resource Group of GAFCON*
FWC	*The Faith we confess: An exposition of the 39 Articles – Gerald Bray*
TPG	*The True Profession of the Gospel: Augustus Toplady and Reclaiming our Reformed Foundations – Lee Gatiss*

Latimer Publications

www.ingramcontent.com/pod-product-compliance
Ingram Content Group UK Ltd.
Pitfield, Milton Keynes, MK11 3LW, UK
UKHW041828200726
13854UKWH00002BA/874

9 780946 307746